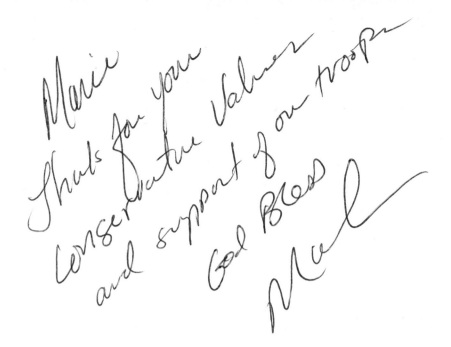

Marie
Thanks for your
conservative values
and support of our troops

God Bless

Mark

A Night with Saddam

D0288484

A Night with Saddam

Mark E. Green MD

ISBN 978-0-557-15320-6

To the medics of 160th Special Operations Aviation Regiment (Airborne) and their families. Your tireless and unwavering service to our nation and the aviators, crews, and support personnel of "The Unit" has been instrumental in the success of the Global War on Terror, and your assistance to me during my brief assignment was THE key to my success.

War is an ugly thing, but not the ugliest of things: the decayed and degraded state of moral and patriotic feeling which thinks that nothing is worth war is much worse. A man who has nothing for which he is willing to fight; nothing he cares about more than his own personal safety; is a miserable creature who has no chance of being free, unless made and kept so by the exertions of better men than himself.

—John Stuart Mill

People sleep peaceably in their beds at night because rough men stand ready to do violence on their behalf.

—George Orwell

A Few Words of Thanks

The environment of Special Forces is unique. Many of our nation's greatest secrets were revealed to me as I signed into the 160th Special Operations Aviation Regiment, otherwise called Task Force 160 or just plain SOAR (pronounced just like it looks). This book is written to bring credit and recognition to the incredible sacrifice of so many in Special Operations and Special Forces, but especially the medics of the 160th SOAR. It is important that people understand the sacrifice and commitment of our Special Operations soldiers, aviators, and medical personnel. Further, the many questions I asked Saddam Hussein on the night of his capture have never been discussed, and many of his answers that night contradict what historians previously reported. I feel that sharing the details of my interview with Saddam Hussein on the night of his capture is an essential piece of history that needs to be published.

I endeavored to keep the nation's secrets held tight while telling this story. That challenge was difficult. If a section seems vague, understand that I could not compromise missions and the men who executed them. How targets are taken down is not in this work. If you want a tactical blow by blow, you need to look elsewhere. This book will focus on the medical aspects of the operations more than anything. I use only the soldiers' first names. It is unnecessary to give their entire name because none of them serve for recognition, but they all love it when it comes their way. And if I am fortunate to have one of them read the book, they will know of whom I am speaking.

I need to thank an ancient Night Stalker for encouraging me to write this book. Myron was retired from the unit when 9/11 occurred. He was flying cushy civilian MEDEVAC choppers in middle Kentucky. Soon after 9/11, he was on the phone with the commander of the unit. With special permission, his old butt was allowed to return to active duty and the 160th Special Operations Aviation Regiment. I flew my first training mission in the 160th with him, a live fire training exercise, or "hit" on an U.S. Army facility in Indiana. Later, we would spend a great deal of time together in Iraq. After I got out of the army, Myron came by the hospital where I was working as a civilian ER doc and asked me, "Where the hell is that book of yours, doc?" I am certain that many of my civilian medical counterparts were a bit befuddled watching this crotchety old aviator and his former flight surgeon hug each other's necks. But combat produces a heart connection between soldiers that cannot be rivaled. Many have attempted to describe the bonds of brotherhood forged in battle, but few have succeeded. But the twinkle in Myron's eye gave me the go ahead I needed to put pen to paper. This would not be written if it were not for his and many other Night Stalkers prodding me to do so. Thanks, Myron, for your unbelievable service to our nation, your friendship, and encouragement. NSDQ.

I also want to thank great friends and colleagues, Troy Harris, John Shields, Jeff Moe, Dale Wallace, and Kevin Blackwell for encouragement and input. Troy was working in the ER when Myron came in. He heard a few bits and pieces of the story and then never let it rest. For the next few months, he kept badgering me to write the story—so thanks Troy. John, thanks for your proofing of the early editions and your encouragement to bring this to print. Dale, an attorney in the literary agent world, gave a great deal of encouragement in the early editions. Jeff, as a busy executive, I never expected the detailed analysis you gave me and can never thank you enough for your insight and advice. Kevin, my best friend from high school and also a busy executive, was a great advisor in the final stages of the project and helped with the final two editions. Thanks, Kevin. I would also like to thank Stephen Mansfield, author of *The Faith of George Bush* and *The Faith of Barack Obama*. Stephen served more as a mentor than editor during the process. As a *New York Times*-bestselling author, Stephen's insight was invaluable.

John Kelly Hewitt, a dear friend and brother in a sense, also served as a strong encourager and proofreader. John Kelly's greatest contribution, however, was introducing me to Shannon. Shannon Dunn served as my copy editor and poured over the manuscript with a microscope. Shannon also kept me encouraged as the project waned into its latter stages. Only I put more hours into this project than Shannon. I am humbled by her assistance and her belief in the need to tell this story.

I want to thank my wife for following me around the United States as a soldier and then as an army physician. No single person has changed me more than Camie, and I am forever in her debt for the sacrifices she has made for our nation and me. The wives sit at home and watch the news with excitement and dread. Excitement comes with the ownership of the mission. The overwhelming majority believes wholeheartedly in the mission and are committed to the service their husbands give the nation. Dread, of course, because the stakes are so very high. The moment they hear of a helicopter crash, they go into a numb state and wait to see if the white vans pull into their driveway. Meanwhile, the children play, unknowing in some other part of the house and not really understanding why their mother has suddenly gotten so quiet. People who have not endured that agony can never fully understand it. I have only witnessed it from the sideline. Waiting to know if the love of your life, the provider of your security, and the father of your children is dead on a foreign battlefield is a necessary evil to the war we fight. Unfortunately, these women rarely get recognized for enduring this stress. Camie, all the other Lady Night Stalkers, and the wives, husbands, fathers, mothers, sons, and daughters of other soldiers, I thank you for your service to our nation.

Lastly, and for this story most importantly, I want to thank the medical platoon of 160th Special Operations Aviation Regiment. The SOAR medics were my constant companions. They trained me on the aircraft and the uniqueness of trauma management in the back of a blacked out helicopter. I taught them some of the latest medications and trauma techniques I acquired in my emergency medicine residency. Together, we followed the Special Operations aviators all over the world and provided better trauma care than on any street in any city in the United States. These guys were diligent in their medical studies, meticulous in their combat planning, and unflinching in the most demanding combat situations. Their courage under fire ranks with the best of our nation's past warriors. Night Stalker Medics often deployed longer and more frequently than the aviators because there were proportionally so few of them. Their service to this country has been unprecedented and deserving of the highest recognition our nation can give.

Because this story is from my perspective, I must tell the readers a little about myself. For some, this might seem as if my purpose for publication is a degree of personal recognition. I want to be clear that I started putting this all together with the initial intent of having a story for my children to read. As the pen flowed on paper, I realized that Myron was right, and the things Hussein said to me needed recording for historical purposes. As I devised a way to take this part of the story to the masses, I felt that also telling the story of a few of the medics with whom I had served, their service, and the challenges they encountered could accomplish multiple objectives. Still, this is my experience, and the book relates things I did and the history God allowed me to be a part of. While I am as addicted to the praise of others just as much as the next person, this book was not intended for that purpose.

For the record, this story is as I remember it and from my perspective only. I admit that many of the assumptions I make about how intelligence data was gathered or processed reflects my limited perspective as a physician planning the medical portion of the operations. This narrative is from my memory, prodded by the journals I kept on each deployment. It is as true as I can recall. Nothing is added and nothing embellished upon. If there are inaccuracies, then it is either my memory or my perspective that has failed the reader. But as I present the stories, I honestly believe this is how it all happened.

A Night with Saddam - Contents

Chapter One

The Capture

Rob, a Special Operations aviation medic, was shaking me out of an unconscious state. My sleep patterns were usually destroyed near the end of a rotation, and waking was almost as challenging as falling asleep. Apparently, some great new intelligence had pinpointed the Ace of Spades, the top of America's list of fifty-two most wanted Iraqi bad guys. Members of the elite Task Force 121 were off to do another hit to get Saddam Hussein. Midway through the hunt for Hussein, the missions brought a sense of complacency because the ones before had all ended the same. A few nobodies were taken from the target, interrogated, and then released. This time it was different. The Special Operations Task Force had taken down an escalating level of key people, whom we believed were ever closer to Saddam.

It began with the capture of Saddam's supposed girlfriend. Rob and I served as the paramedic and emergency physician, respectively, in an MH-60 K, a Special Operations version of the army's workhorse Black Hawk helicopter. The Black Hawk had the capacity to carry eleven combat-equipped soldiers and was armed with twin 7.62 mm miniguns, each with a 4,000-rounds-per-minute rate of fire. For this mission, we sat on standby at our facility at Baghdad International Airport (BIAP). While these standby missions were the easiest for us, they were also the least exciting.

We threw our gear in the back of the "hooptie" and headed to the flight line. How our Nissan pickup got the name hooptie was apparently at a level above my top secret special compartmented intelligence security clearance. We drove five hundred yards from our sleeping area down to the flight line at BIAP, loaded our gear onto the chopper, turned on the auxiliary power unit (APU), a small jet engine that allowed for a rapid start up, and waited to see if the operators took any casualties. As I recall, this mission was very close to BIAP, and the operators drove to the target. I sat in the helo waiting for the call for a CASEVAC, or casualty evacuation.

No call came, and at the completion of the mission, the assault bird designated as the medical evacuation aircraft—still loaded with all our medical equipment as well as with its medical crew, Rob, and I—"stood down." Our Special Operations aircraft could easily be configured with medical equipment and "converted" from an assault platform carrying just shooters to a medical aircraft or both. I always passed through the 160th Special Operations Aviation Regiment's TOC, or Tactical Operations Center, after these missions. The SOAR TOC provided command and control of the aircraft portion of the battle whenever the special operators used our aircraft to do assaults, or hits. As I passed through this night, joking with the guys in the TOC and grabbing some of the sergeant major's nasty coffee, I was met by one of the operators, who was looking for the medical officer. He handed me a bag full of medications and said the woman taken from the target, supposedly Hussein's girlfriend, revealed that the medications were Saddam Hussein's. They wanted my analysis on them and any hard intelligence, or intel, they might give on his health.

The bag, similar to a one-gallon zipper lock bag, was full of several different kinds of antihypertensive medications. We expected this. Intel had told us all along that the Ace of Spades had high blood pressure. I even carried nitroglycerin and other cardiac meds during hits to get Hussein in the event the excitement of a capture caused him to have the big one. We did not want to spend months and millions of dollars tracking this guy down only to have him die of a coronary during capture. I also noticed a significant quantity of the little blue pills the pharmaceutical company Pfizer sells for erectile dysfunction. Seems Saddam was quite the Viagra junkie. Once the operator showed me a picture of Hussein's girlfriend, I understood the need for the Viagra. I guess a guy on the run from Task Force 121 can't be too choosey. I gave my report on the meds and left the TOC.

Some days later, the pace began to quicken, and a hit was done to grab Saddam's secretary. I never knew if the girlfriend provided the intelligence that led to the secretary or not. We like to assume it did. But this guy turned out to be a very interesting character. The hit was done way out west, and the operators needed all the SOAR aircraft. My medical team—this time myself, a paramedic from the army's Special Operations counter-terrorism unit, and an air force flight surgeon who looked thirteen—boarded an MH-53 Pave Low and flew in a separate formation to an airfield near the target.

The MH-53 Pave Low is a modernized and specially outfitted version of the HH-53, which first saw action in the Vietnam War. Great air force Special Ops pilots fly the MH-53s in support of Joint Special Operations Command missions. But us army guys felt there was no comparison to flying with our Night Stalkers. OK, so we were biased. Whenever the medics got bumped to the Air Force birds, we mumbled under our breath, but were still insanely appreciative of the opportunity to be a part of the missions. We often joked that joining the air force guys was also a great opportunity to prepare for the transition to the civilian world. Interservice rivalry is a great thing, and we always got as much as we gave. My fellow Night Stalkers and I were proud to serve with all the U.S. Air Force Special Ops pilots.

When the missions were remote from our base of operations, the medical aircraft, along with some escort, often flew to a field near the target so we could quickly respond if an operator was wounded. Again, we would sit there either with helicopter's blades turning or with the APU running, ready to go. Whenever this scenario occurred, we would attempt to `insert a SOAR medic into one of the assault aircraft along with the shooters, to have at least one medical guy actually on the target. This duty fell to Rob, who gladly took the call.

Rob had been a Night Stalker Medic since Moses was a private. He was a large man with a booming voice, who from the look of him, did not appear to be the Special Operations type. However, I soon found out that appearances were deceiving. Rob's reputation in the unit was anchored by his rescue of a downed pilot from a burning aircraft. For that action, which was not in combat but in a training accident years before, he was awarded a Soldier's Medal and a great deal of respect from his fellow Night Stalkers. When I arrived at the 160th SOAR, Rob was undergoing a difficult divorce. His wife at the time was not capable of handling the incredible absences he and the other Night Stalkers were undergoing to fight the terrorists. His commitment to the freedom of the nation and his oath to defend her was resolute. Rob's spouse's inability to tolerate the absences caused a considerable amount of bitterness, which she took out on him in a variety of ways. Rob bore the brunt of fighting an enemy and the heartache of losing his wife as a casualty of defending the nation. Many young women fell into the same pattern, especially as the war continued – it was just one of the many consequences and costs of the combat.

There was a casualty on this particular mission; a female on the target had been hit in the lower leg by the bullet of an enemy AK-47 assault rifle. Rob, who was positioned on an assault aircraft, took care of the patient. Rob was an extremely competent paramedic. His decision making for both trauma and medical conditions was one of the best in the medical platoon that served the aviators of 160th SOAR. His procedural skills were also excellent. Another Night Stalker medic nearly lost his ear on a training airborne jump. Apparently, this soldier's risers, the straps connecting his harness to the parachute, slapped into the back of his ear lobe, nearly slicing it off. Rob sutured the cartilage and skin as well as any doctor could have. The repair was outstanding.

The female hit on this target had a bullet penetrate her lower leg, hit the tibia, or the larger of the two bones in the lower leg, and then exit just above where it entered. Rob splinted her, controlled the hemorrhage by placing a pressure bandage, then started fluids and antibiotics through an IV.

When I arrived back at our base area following the mission, I meandered over to the battlefield interrogation facility (BIF). The battlefield interrogation facility was a modified jail where high-value targets captured by our Special Operations task force were held and interrogated prior to turning them over to the main "prisoner system" used by the regular army. At this point in the deployment, I was the only doctor covering the entire Special Operations task force. This left me with the unenviable task of giving the physical exams to the detainees, many of whom had no concept of personal hygiene. These physicals were one of the first things that happened to them on their arrival to the BIF and prior to any interrogations. I was escorted into the interrogation room, where I met a gentleman whom the operators and military intelligence guys manning the BIF called Hussein's secretary. He had apparently been caught with a large sum of cash and had his suitcases packed for Syria.

He was a frumpy looking fellow of about 5 feet, 6 inches with a portly belly. His absence of shoes and scruffy hair made me think of a hobbit. We maintained sanity by giving these guys nicknames when we did the physicals. Most of the captured high-value targets or detainees were petrified; the most elite soldiers in the history of the world had just pulled them off a target in the middle of the night. I attempted to treat the detainees with great respect when doing the physical exam. In most cases, as would be the case later with the Ace of Spades himself, my being a doctor seemed to relax the detainees, and they often opened up. This guy was no exception, and he quickly smiled and started telling me all about himself. I had no special feelings for detainees, but they seemed to be glad to speak with someone who was not attempting to extract information. It was an interesting dynamic.

Several days later, my medics and I were watching television in our aid station when a call came from the BIF. Apparently, the hobbit had passed out. The interrogator on the line giving us the report was obviously freaked out and was yelling, "We can't get a pulse!" My two medics and I grabbed our aid bags and made a mad dash to the interrogation facility. When we entered the room, the hobbit was on the floor, and an interrogator was attempting CPR. I distinctly recall the vision of the interrogator giving mouth-to-mouth resuscitation and thinking, "Now that's what I call service." The medics got an IV started and hooked him to a cardiac monitor. Rob intubated him, placing a tube in his trachea, which allowed us to breathe for him using a bag hooked to an oxygen bottle. The cardiac monitor showed that the patient had electrical activity in his heart's conduction system, but his heart muscle fibers were not contracting in a synchronized fashion, thus not generating a pulse. In medical terms, the patient had pulseless electrical activity (PEA). There are numerous medical causes for PEA. This detainee had no signs of physical abuse or trauma, so we proceeded with a likely cardiac cause. I gave him a dose of epinephrine and atropine, drugs listed in the American Heart Association's algorithm for treating this condition, as well as intravenous fluids and we loaded him on a stretcher. All the while we were continuing to breathe for him and do CPR chest compressions.

Lou, the chief medical administrator for the Special Operations headquarters over our unit, was there watching the scene unfold and volunteered to drive us to the forward surgical team's emergency department, about 1.5 miles from our current location. We tossed the medical gear and the stretcher-bound hobbit into a green Volkswagen van. Immediately, Lou shot off the starting line. I should say he shot off the pole position, because unbeknownst to my medics and me, Lou was a NASCAR junkie and wannabe. It was all we could do to keep the oxygen flowing to the patient as we rattled about in the back of the van like dice in a Yahtzee cup.

When we got Hussein's secretary into the tiny ER, the forward area surgical team was eager to help. This small facility was staffed by a group of surgeons, and knowing I was an ER-trained doc, they were more than willing to let me manage the cardiac code. The patient remained in PEA, and we moved through the advanced cardiac life support algorithm designed by the American Heart Association to treat this condition. After about thirty minutes with no pulse, and with the patient beginning to turn purple, I asked to use their ultrasound machine. I did so more to show my medics the value of the machine. When I placed the probe on his chest, his heart was still attempting to contract and the individual muscle fibers were seen on the black and white screen not working in the synchronized manner necessary to produce a pulse. Instead of calling time of death, I decided to keep trying. We pushed more fluids and more drugs, and in about ten minutes, one of the medics checked for a pulse at the femoral artery at the top of the patient's thigh. To our surprise, he had one. Another look with the ultrasound machine proved what was suspected: the hobbit had a heart beat, a pulse, and was now generating a measurable blood pressure. When the ultrasound machine revealed cardiac activity, but no pulse, it prompted me to continue the resuscitation. What better advertisement for battlefield ultrasound can you get?

As was necessary in this case, we started the patient on medications designed to strengthen his heart and his blood vessels and to keep blood flowing to the vital organs. The interrogators and intelligence people soon arrived to ensure the identity of the person remained undisclosed. They were helpful in securing a MEDEVAC helicopter to fly from the FAST team's rudimentary ER over to the main combat support hospital, where Saddam's secretary would be placed in an ICU.

Days later, the interrogators told us that the hobbit awakened on his second day in the ICU and was taken off the ventilator. Laboratory results were conclusive that he had had a cardiac event, which probably led to his cardiac arrest the day prior. He was grateful that we had saved his life, and showed his gratitude by giving them some needed intelligence. Unfortunately, while we were able to save his brain by the continuous CPR, the lab data showed that the lengthy resuscitation had deprived his kidneys of needed oxygen, leading to kidney failure. The interrogators also told us that no US medical unit had dialysis capability, so the U.S. Army turned him over to the local Iraqi hospital for dialysis. Dialysis was necessary to regulate toxins and electrolytes normally cleared by the kidneys. We later learned the Iraqi's either did not have the ability to dialyze him or chose not to do so. He subsequently died of complications of his kidney failure. Fortunately, he had given the intel to our interrogators, and we were off chasing the next piece of the puzzle. And the next piece of the puzzle required the medics and me to fly outside of our comfort zone.

Special Operations aviation was a high-demand asset. Because our pilots were trained to do tasks no other pilots were trained to do, demand for our aircraft and pilots meant we often needed to be augmented by regular army aviation assets. At this point in Operation Iraqi Freedom, these non-Special Operations helicopters were not equipped with antimissile capabilities. When assigned to support the Special Operations aviation unit, the guys often got fairly routine missions like picking up supplies or friendly people. Flying with them, after you are accustomed to the best-equipped choppers flown by the most elite aviators in the history of the world, can produce a significant degree of consternation. Occasionally, the Special Operations ground force commander, our customers, would request all SOAR aircraft assets for an assault, which meant the medical team was required to ride with the regular army guys augmenting our task force. Not to denigrate the regular army pilots, but their level of training and the sophistication of the aircraft they flew were no match for the Night Stalkers. The regular army pilots were no less heroic and their contributions no less valuable. They simply were not as experienced and were not trained the way Night Stalker pilots were trained. I recall that as a regular army, or non-Special Operations infantry officer, there was always a sense that the spec ops guys thought a little too highly of themselves. Now serving in Special Operations, I realized the mission and the training were significantly different. While I would never devalue the contribution of either—regular army people took Baghdad, after all—the difference in skill sets did produce a degree of cautious concern when we flew with the regular army guys and gals.

Shortly after bagging the secretary, we got a call saying Saddam's personal physician was found by one of the army spec ops units. We were told to go get him and bring him to the Battle Field Interrogation Facility on our compound for questioning. Our unit preferred to question the higher value detainees itself prior to conducting missions. The task force's SOAR assets were needed elsewhere, so the mission fell to the regular army augmentees. There was some concern over the health of Saddam's physician, so I was asked to fly with them in the event he needed medical attention in flight. Because adrenaline causes an increase in a person's heart rate, and thus increases the demand for oxygen for the rapidly beating heart muscle, it is akin to a form of cardiac stress test that a person might take at a cardiologist's office. I did not want to chance the stress of this flight leading to a cardiac arrest. Putting this guy in a Black Hawk and flying him through the Tikrit area of operation was going to increase his heart rate; it certainly did mine.

This mission was planned for early morning, which meant flying in broad daylight. And to add insult to injury, we would be flying less than one mile from where a Black Hawk was shot down just weeks before. Saddam's well-informed physician, who we were collecting that morning, would be aware of the danger. His elevated heart rate could easily lead to a heart attack. Thus, my presence on the aircraft was essential. I was a bit pensive throughout the flight, but not quite to the level of a cardiac stress test. I was not without the thought that I may be the one needing attention. But after logging a few uninterrupted hours of flight time along the great Tigress and Euphrates Rivers, we were safe back home with the Ace of Spades's medical doctor.

As a physician in Special Operations, my security clearance was very high. However, many of the enemy intelligence details remained outside my purview. Consequently, I never knew if the progression of takedowns from girlfriend to secretary to doctor were ever tied together. But for me, it seemed we were getting closer and closer. The briefings certainly took on an energy level suggesting such. All of the Task Force 121 planning personnel in the Joint Operations Center seemed keyed up during the first weeks of December.

Meanwhile, back in Mississippi, my father, a Southern Baptist preacher, began to think that if we could capture Saddam, the whole thing would implode and the soldiers and, more importantly to him, his son could come home. This prompted my dad to send a letter to all of his fellow ministers in his county. The letter asked them to fast and pray all day long on Friday, December 12. On that Friday, my mother and father fasted and prayed that God would allow the soldiers to capture Saddam and, my mother added to her prayer, that God would allow her son to be a part of the mission.

I came to life after a good shaking from Rob and looked at my watch. It was early afternoon on Saturday, December 13, 2004. He informed me that the MH-53 Pave Lows were arriving in thirty minutes and we would be flying a MEDEVAC mission. He said the ground guys were certain this would be the hit that got the Ace of Spades. We were told the phone lines were disconnected and that a C-130 was on standby to fly him out of the country if necessary. It was not routine for the JOC to kill our phone lines. Something very serious was going on.

We launched at 1500 hours Zulu, or 1800 hours, 6 PM local time, and flew directly to an airfield in the vicinity of Tikrit, Saddam's hometown. As was our standard procedure, we sat at the airfield with blades turning, listening to the play-by-play of the operators. The U.S. Army's Special Operations force is the most disciplined of all the nation's elite warriors. Others might say they are the most anally retentive. However, considering the degree of accuracy demanded by their job description, and that a mistake could easily mean another flag-draped coffin, who can blame them?

When executing missions, they used key words to signify the completion of a phase of operations. For example, if a certain building has been breached and cleared, they may pass the code word "Dallas" or "Buffalo" over the net. This mission extended longer than we thought it should, and it seemed from the use of the code words that the operators were going back over the same ground, searching again for signs. Then we heard a call over the net saying, "We have Jackpot." The JOC operations officer managing the battle asked for clarification, and an excited operator said, "We've got Jackpot." At that point, the admiral commanding TF-121, who after countless missions with the unit had never been heard on the radio said,

"Do you mean Big Jackpot?" The answer was, "Yes, we have Big Jackpot."

In our haste to get on the birds and make the mission, we never got the detailed intel report we normally do before these type of missions. It turns out that Saddam's cook was known to be on the target. We thought perhaps that Hussein would be there as well. So Little Jackpot was the cook, and Big Jackpot was Hussein. The Ace of Spades, Big Jackpot, was now in custody. An MH-6 Little Bird pilot with 160th SOAR was then called in to get the HVT, or high-value target. As he landed on the objective, an operator loaded a hooded man onto his Little Bird, and they both flew to a special operator's compound on a nearby airfield. My buddy thought he had the cook on board. Later, when he realized who he had just flown off the target, he was a bit taken aback. That pilot would, the following January, sit with Laura Bush at the president's State of the Union address.

Because our primary responsibility was providing medical coverage to the operators on the target, Rob, my medic, and I remained on the medical aircraft while the ground guys continued to clear the target. By the time we returned to our Task Force area, the Ace of Spades was secured in our battlefield interrogation facility (BIF). A recently arrived Special Operations medical officer was now responsible for the physical exams of the high-value targets. He, a bald ER doctor, made the famous medical exam shown all over the world on CNN. Had he not arrived only a few days prior, I would have done that exam.

When we returned to our base, Rob was called to the BIF, asked to get an EKG, and told to shave Hussein. I and another SOAR medic stationed with us took care of the gear, cleaning everything and putting away the equipment. At this point, I began a short-lived debate in my head about going to the BIF to try to get a glimpse of Hussein. I knew this was a historic moment. I recall telling myself, "Mark, if you don't go over there, you will regret it for the rest of your life." But I needed to ready my gear because my ride to the United States was arriving the following day. However, the weight of the moment in history compelled me to go. I followed the well-trodden path from our medical building to the BIF. Having worked with the interrogators for a few months, I was well known by them and the guards at the facility and thus allowed in, even though no longer primarily responsible for the medical care of the prisoners there. I sat just outside Hussein's door as a parade of people came and went, getting their photo taken with this man who, as the president of Iraq, had terrorized and killed so many people. The weight of the moment began to settle in on me. Few people in the history of mankind have been as horrible as Saddam Hussein. I realized that a comparable point in history might have been the capture of Adolph Hitler, had that actually occurred. Since it had not, this moment seemed even larger to me.

There was very little interrogating going on at this late hour in the BIF. Most of the intelligence people wanted him to rest prior to their intense questioning. The dignitaries and senior commanders had visited him and were now gone. About this time, around midnight, the physician assigned to the BIF left. One of the senior intelligence officers recognized me standing outside the cell speaking with the interpreters and told me that the admiral wanted a medical officer with Saddam constantly. He asked if I would go in and stay the first night with him. I said yes and gathered my thoughts. The shear excitement of the moment was balanced by the realization of the terror and evil this man had produced in his lifetime. I grabbed a worn-out copy of the *Stars and Stripes* newspaper and walked into his makeshift cell to share in the first night of captivity with the captured King of Babylon. Seems my mom's prayer was answered.

Chapter Two

Becoming a Night Stalker

As coincidence would have it, I signed in to my new unit, the 160th Special Operations Aviation Regiment (SOAR) — the Night Stalkers — on the one-year anniversary of September 11, 2001. Mark Bowden's book and the subsequent movie, *Black Hawk Down*, focused on the actions of this elite Special Operations unit. At age thirty-seven and, at that point, after twelve years of service to the army, my life in the Special Operations community was about to begin. After entering the "compound," I walked toward the headquarters building to sign in. The compound is a secured facility inside the secured military post, sort of a fenced secret area inside the fenced post. Going through layers of security added to the mystique of the place and gave me a sense of elation at being selected to be a part of this elite force.

As I walked from my car to the headquarters building of the unit, I noticed a large group of soldiers and family members gathered around the Night Stalker Memorial for the anniversary service for 9/11. Nearing the service, I could hear the commander announcing the names of the Night Stalkers who had died in the past year fighting the War on Terror. Nine in all, more than any other unit in the army at that point, had given their lives in this fight. Imagine joining an elite Special Operations unit, walking on for your first day of duty, and literally stumbling into a service commemorating the fallen soldiers who had sacrificed their lives in the War on Terror. I knew joining this organization would bring me close to the fight. My wife and I had spoken of it as we considered joining the 160th. But as I reported for duty to the unit that day, I had no idea the ceremony was planned, and the coincidence of it happening as I walked up to join the outfit was a sobering thought. As had happened many times before, I asked, "What have I gotten myself into?"

My other options would seem to most people to be far more appealing. As a graduate of an emergency medicine residency, the number of lucrative positions for an emergency medicine physician exceeded the supply. Having chosen to be an army emergency physician, I had already taken a significant pay cut relative to my civilian counterparts. But life in an army ER would not be bad. Working seventeen shifts a month leaves several days to moonlight for extra dollars or for quality time with the family. Other military units were also available to me. Their reduced hours and certainly reduced risk to life and limb were attractive. Instead, I had chosen to serve alongside soldiers who would expose themselves to more enemy fire than any other unit in the army and have more frequent deployments, all for less pay.

In light of this, it may seem my choices were completely selfless; they were not. The 160th Special Operations pilots are absolutely the best helicopter pilots in the world. I knew I would be going to war; it was inevitable. I knew that choosing the 160th would place me closer to the action. But knowing I would be flying with the very best gave me a sense of security and safety that made the choice to join this unit, although counterintuitive, self-protective. There was also a strong patriotic pull on my heart. My father and two of his brothers had served the nation. But still, arriving at the unit during a memorial ceremony would cause anyone to say, "What have I gotten myself into?" Or more accurately, "Why did God put me here at this point in time?"

Then, as a part of the ceremony, the chaplain took the podium. He talked of the attack one year ago, and essentially, he rendered a sermon not unlike what one would hear on any given Southern Baptist Sunday morning. For me, it brought on a rush of thoughts. The conservative nature of the army, which allows for "In God we trust" to remain in all they do, was immediately evident. What company in America could have a chaplain preach a sermon on such a memorial? Everywhere else across the country, leaders of such services—if praying at all—were doing so to an unnamed entity for fear of offending someone. Not here—and the resistance to take God out of all we do made me feel proud of the army.

The chaplain's words also brought me back to my young days as an infantry company commander in the famed 82nd Airborne Division. While in command, an event occurred that I often recalled over the years when life in the army frustrated me for whatever reason. Our unit was a week away from completing our time on the immediate recall status of the RDF, or rapid deployment force. The 82nd Airborne Division always has a brigade of infantryman, nearly four-thousand soldiers, ready to go in eighteen hours. For the leaders and most of the men, that means being within thirty minutes of the base. Living day in and day out in a perimeter thirty minutes from your office is painful. I was fatigued from being on such a tight string, unable even to go out for a nice dinner in Raleigh. Soldiers were in Somalia, but the incident depicted in Bowden's book *Black Hawk Down* had not yet occurred. There was some chance we could be deployed, but it was unlikely.

Sometime in the last week on RDF, I remember being at a grocery store and getting side-tracked watching people pile their shopping carts high with food. I thought of the hunger, death, and fighting for food shown so vividly in Somalia. And the frustration of being on the short recall ebbed away. As I had been reminded so often before, it was our service in the army that brought peace to our people and allowed for such great prosperity at the hands of ingenious Americans. In fact, helping to preserve that peace was my primary reason for giving my life to the military. Reminders like these are cherished whenever they present themselves.

The chaplain also took some time to describe the events on September 11, 2001.

Prior to the attack, Osama bin Laden was a name recognized by few Americans, despite his involvement in several previous attacks on U.S. interests. Unlike the infamous attack by the empire of Japan, there were no daily conversations about a coming war with Al Qaeda. Plainly put, America was sucker punched. It came from a people who, for reasons unfathomable to us, deeply hated us. As the chaplain continued, I knew the festering hatred of radical Islam in madrasas around the world ensured that we were still far from peace. This fight was long from over, round two would soon start, and I wanted to do my duty and serve in whatever capacity God allowed.

After the ceremony, I walked to the commander's office to officially report for duty. He voiced his pleasure at having a former infantry officer as his doctor. Normally physicians with go-to-war units are fresh out of their internship. Their only military experience is a few weeks in a gentleman's version of an officer's basic training and a couple of months serving as medical students in army hospitals. I had graduated from West Point in 1986 and served over nine years as an infantryman. It was my thinking then that, if you cannot fly, why serve in the air force? The logical extension was, if you are in the army, why not be an infantryman and a Ranger? After completing a stint of schools at Fort Benning, Georgia, which included graduating from the U.S. Army Ranger School, I moved to Fort Knox, Kentucky, for my first duty assignment. Over the next four years of my first tour of duty as an infantry officer, I served first as a rifle platoon leader, the direct leader of thirty-five infantrymen. I left that position to become the battalion scout platoon leader, and later I served as a principal staff officer, the battalion personnel officer responsible for all human resource functions for an eight hundred–plus man infantry battalion.

While assigned to the mechanized infantry battalion at Fort Knox, I developed a strong desire to join the Rangers. I considered myself to be a "Ranger qualified" officer but not a true Ranger. It was my opinion that to be a Ranger, you had to have worn the scroll, the unit patch indicating you were assigned to the Ranger unit. All army infantry officers are sent to the Army's Ranger School at Fort Benning, Georgia. The school is a right of passage. Many do not make it through this arduous course. But to me, doing so did not mean I was an army Ranger. I spoke on numerous occasions with my sergeant major, a former Ranger and the highest-ranking enlisted man in the battalion, regarding my potential to make it into the Ranger regiment. He gave me high marks and felt I would be successful. I ultimately opted not to compete for a position. I was recently married and wanted to spend that first year working on my marriage, not working on my army career. That decision, while the best for my wife and me, began a series of missed opportunities as a soldier. Shortly after I would have arrived to the Rangers, they deployed to combat operations in Panama as a part of Operation Just Cause. In my juvenile and unlearned state as a young infantry lieutenant, this event left me with considerable regret for not attempting to join them.

Most nonmilitary people struggle to understand this emotion. Frequently, people outside the military see this desire to go to war in our soldiers and classify all soldiers as warmongers. What many people mean when they say warmonger is a person who has a lust for killing. Soldiers are not warmongers. The young soldier who never experienced combat does not want to take life. Further, he or she realizes that going means others who are close to you may die. The soldier simply wants to know if he has what it takes. Combat is seen as an ultimate challenge. War is the extreme of man versus man, and for those who trained for years to be a soldier in combat, finding out that you can survive and succeed is a bizarre yearning. I realize that the analogy is not perfect, but no football player wants to train his entire life never to play in the game and know that he has what it takes. A favorite author of mine, John Eldredge, speaks of the way men behave. He attributes our "wild heart" to the way God built us. John says, "Every man wants to play the hero." Others might suggest some evolutionary benefit from our years as hunter-gatherers. But clearly in most men there exists, as Eldredge puts it, "the desire to win a great battle." Why else do we spend billions on professional sports and movies like *Brave Heart* and *Gladiator*? We want to win a great battle.

Courage under fire is the ultimate goal. But for most of the people I knew, fear of death was never even an afterthought. For me, my greatest fear was not that some stray Iraqi bullet would make my wife a widow. My greatest fear, and I believe that of most of the professional special operators with whom I served, was fear of failure. The last thing we wanted was to let our brothers in arms down. The fear of failure pushed the fear of death to the recesses of almost all of our minds.

Having missed the opportunity in Panama, I requested and was fortunate enough to get assigned to the famed 82nd Airborne Division, based at Fort Bragg, North Carolina. Before reporting, I had to attend the six-month advanced infantry officer training. This course prepared you to be a staff officer and infantry company commander in charge of nearly 150 soldiers. While in the school, Saddam Hussein invaded Kuwait. The 82nd Airborne Division was sent immediately and was the first United States military unit to land in Saudi Arabia. They were President Bush 41's "line in the sand." As a light infantry unit, the other units in the army were calling it the speed bump in the sand. Soon, the buildup brought Desert Shield to a formidable force. Near the end of my infantry officer's advanced training, Desert Shield converted to Desert Storm, and this extremely eager infantry officer got to watch the war on CNN. Again, it was a missed opportunity to test the skills as an infantry leader and soldier.

I reported for duty at Fort Bragg, North Carolina just as the 82nd Airborne Division was returning from combat. Talk about a leadership challenge. Imagine you are the only infantry officer in an entire infantry battalion with no combat infantryman's badge. In the 82nd, I served as an airborne rifle company commander and battalion budget and supply officer. While I was in command, the United States sent forces to Somalia to safeguard food shipments. Again the army chose another unit, and I missed a third chance to know whether I had what it takes. Following my command, I served as an assignments officer at the Corps HQ in hopes of getting a chance to command the Corps' long-range surveillance company. I interviewed for the job and was offered the position. Before actually taking the job, my wife and I made a decision that had been brewing for some time. I informed the brigade commander that I decided to get out of the army and go to medical school instead. I called Department of the Army's personnel command responsible for assigning infantry officers and accepted a recruiting command in a town where there was a medical school. Our family moved to Dayton, Ohio, I assumed command of a company of army recruiters, took the medical school prerequisite courses at night, and I was eventually accepted to medical school in Dayton. During my command of the recruiting company, the fighting in Somalia escalated. I recall watching the reports of the special operators and aviators of 160th SOAR after the events chronicled in *Black Hawk Down*. All I could say was, "I've missed again." Although I was attending medical school on an army scholarship, the possibility that my future would include going to war with a unit as covert as 160th SOAR was not a remote cognitive thought.

Many people over the years since have asked me why an army Airborne Ranger would want to go to medical school. My reasons were many, and I admit some were selfish. My West Point classmate and friend Doug Prevost was assigned as my brigade surgeon while I was in command of an infantry company in the 82nd. He constantly talked about the rewards of medicine. His mission to heal seemed more fulfilling than my mission to train to kill. During this time of relative peace in the world, there seemed little chance I would get to use my infantry skills. I loved soldiers. As an infantry officer advances through the ranks, he often finds himself further and further from the troops. This was less appealing to me. The two professions in the military that worked closely with soldiers throughout their careers were the medical officers and the chaplains. And while I considered the chaplaincy, I just did not feel the call to do it, and knew that it was one job you did not attempt unless divinely summoned. About the same time, my father had a surgery on his esophagus. Shortly after the surgery, his esophagus ruptured in what I now know is a Borhave's, a medical condition that is extremely deadly. He spent forty-two days in an ICU but eventually recovered. Every day, the critical care doctors and surgeons would brief my family.

I unfortunately had missed recent opportunities to use my infantry skills and was competing against other officers with combat experience. Now I was training for some "future" opportunity to test those skills, but these physicians saved my dad's life, and many other people like him, on nearly a daily basis. The effect was galvanizing, and I resolved to get out of the infantry and go to medical school.

After four years of medical school and three years of residency in emergency medicine, I had a decision to make. September 11, 2001, occurred during my senior year of residency, right about the time my classmates and I were deciding on our first assignments as newly trained army ER docs. All the soon-to-be-graduating residents knew war was on the horizon. A friend of mine from my infantry years was assigned to the U.S. Army Special Operations Command and took it upon himself to tell the command surgeon about me. One late afternoon I got a surprise phone call from the U.S. Army Special Operations Command, asking me to consider being a SOCOM medical officer. I was flattered and asked him what he had in mind. He suggested the 160th Special Operations Aviation Regiment. I took the opportunity, completed the "assessment," and was selected to be the flight surgeon for the first battalion, 160th SOAR. Following a few courses on special operations and aviation medicine, I reported to the Night Stalkers.

For me as an "army Ranger" who left the infantry to be a physician, the battle had changed. For years, I trained on the techniques of war. From the individual skills necessary to take life, like marksmanship training, hand-to-hand combat, and the use of the bayonet to the advanced skills of leading a company in combat operations, my entire military career up to starting residency had been about knowing how, to make "the other poor dumb bastard die for his country." In basic training at West Point, I awoke every morning to that famous speech by George C. Scott from the movie *Patton*. It, and what it stands for, is etched forever in my brain. According to John Eldredge, they are hard-wired in my DNA. Now, however, I was trained to save lives, not take them. While I would still carry a rifle as a flight surgeon, my primary tools were meticulously packaged in a medical bag. The dichotomy between the M-4 rifle and the "airway kit," or the tourniquets we carried, made the medics and I in one sense walking contradictions: part warrior and part healer. At the time, I never really gave it much thought. In retrospect, I believe both the warrior and the healer parts of me wanted to be a part of this; I wanted to know if I had what it took to do it, and do it well.

The trip from the memorial ceremony to the commander's office was only a few hundred feet. The words of the chaplain and the notion of the memorial ceremony dominated my thoughts. Entering the outer office, his secretary, the wife of a senior Night Stalker crewmember, took me in to meet LTC Jeff. LTC Jeff was a legend in the Special Operations community and in army aviation. The rumors about him preceded me signing into the unit. In my last months in residency at Fort Hood, Texas, and after being selected to serve as a flight surgeon for the 160th SOAR, I got word that a Night Stalker Little Bird pilot lost his leg in a motorcycle accident and was currently admitted to Brooke Army Medical Center at Fort Sam Houston, San Antonio, Texas. Dana was the pilot of an MH-6 Little Bird, the small insertion platform designed to carry four men into a tight spot. Shortly after returning from combat in Afghanistan, and while riding his motorcycle, Dana was clipped by a drunk driver, grinding the lower portion of his leg underneath his six hundred–pound bike. All efforts to save his leg failed. Visiting him, and introducing myself to him at this time, was awkward for me. But I wanted to reassure him that as his future flight surgeon I would support him flying again should he master his prosthesis. In this early visit, Dana shared a number of stories about the guy who would soon take command of Task Force 160.

It was not only LTC Jeff's flying skills that earned him the respect and admiration of so many warriors. LTC Jeff had commanded at every level in special ops aviation. Dana recounted numerous stories of LTC Jeff's common sense approach to life and leadership. As I was soon to find out, he could reduce the most complex leadership situation into a three-word sentence that rivaled any stand-up comedian in Las Vegas. And the fact that he was always right and never self-serving made his observations EF Hutton–like. Men in the unit, as well as others who had served with this intrepid lieutenant colonel, often quoted his original colloquialisms. While LTC Jeff was the most sacrificial leader I ever met in what ultimately would be sixteen years in the army, he was also the most demanding. His expectations were perfection, and because he was such an endearing personality, everyone wanted to deliver it to him.

But Dana was clear that LTC Jeff's most enduring quality was his "no bullshit, don't screw with my soldiers" mind-set. The army of the early twenty-first century was plagued by a zero-defects mentality. Many leaders worked hard to impress their next higher commander, sometimes never taking risks and rarely telling higher headquarters no, regardless of the mission's stupidity. Not so this battalion commander. He frequently argued with higher headquarters on behalf of the soldiers. That characteristic alone made him loved by the men he commanded. Few men earned genuine respect from the aviators in the Special Operations community. My first impression on that September day synched well with what Dana had prepared me for. Over the coming months, my admiration for and my connection to him grew. I have never worked for a better leader.

As I left the commander's office, I could see a few wives and another small group of people around the 160th SOAR monument located in the center of the compound. The memorial ceremony had ended, but a few stragglers and these women remained. I did not really understand what was going on. The monument lists the names of all fallen Night Stalkers. This group of women, I would later learn, was known as the Gold Star Wives. The Gold Star Wives are the spouses of fallen Night Stalkers, who along with their children, remain forever in the care of the unit. As the new unit surgeon, I would not have to wait long before comforting new members to this organization. I walked to my car and drove home.

Chapter Three

Who Are the Night Stalkers?

The 160th Special Operations Aviation Regiment is the nation's helicopter insertion force for all covert precision antiterrorists units. Whether it is the army's elite special forces or one of the Navy's SEAL teams, none of the U.S. military "spec ops shooters" wants to be placed on a rooftop for an assault by any other aircraft. The unit got its start following the failed attempt to rescue the U.S. hostages seized in Iran. Interestingly, the first mission I planned with the unit would be a hit placing me extremely close to Iranian air space.

In November 1979, radical fundamentalist Muslims stormed and seized the U.S. embassy in Tehran, Iran, taking fifty-two U.S. citizens hostage. Operation Eagle Claw was launched in April 1980. Eight navy RH-53D helicopters launched off the deck of the USS *Nimitz* in the Arabian Sea at the same time six C-130 air force airplanes with a capacity of sixty-five people left Masirah Island, Oman. Both flight groups were to rendezvous six hundred miles into an Iranian no-mans-land known as Desert One. Two of the navy helicopters experienced mechanical problems and aborted. On arrival to Desert One, another was found to be nonoperational. Because mission planners felt a minimum of six aircraft were needed for the mission, the abort decision was made. In the ensuing chaos of refueling and preparing to depart, one of the navy helicopters collided with an air force C-130, killing eight men and injuring many more. The commander of the operation, Colonel Charlie Beckwith loaded all survivors on the C-130s and left the burning hulls and the undamaged helicopters along with the dead. Operation Eagle Claw was an embarrassment to the nation and cost the lives of eight courageous warriors.[1]

A congressional review committee, known as the Holloway Commission, evaluated the planning and execution of Operation Eagle Claw. One critical revelation from the operation was that although the U.S. military establishment had invested great amounts of money and time in developing operators to execute ground attacks with counterterrorism operations, the United States had no Special Operations aviation asset capable of competent night flight. At the conclusion of the commission, the hostages were still held captive in Tehran.

Planning for the second attempt, Operation Honey Badger, began in earnest. This time, Colonel Beckwith's counterterrorism unit went to the U.S. Army, specifically the 101st Airborne Division, looking for pilots. The 101st had flown thousands of helicopter ground assaults during the Vietnam War. In June 1980, only five years after the fall of Saigon, army aviators began an intense training regimen to fly precision helicopter-borne assaults at night using night vision goggles. Task Force 158, the precursor to Task Force 160 and the 160th Special Operations Aviation Regiment, was born.[2]

Over the ensuing years, the army's Special Operations unit, the Night Stalkers, with the motto "Night Stalkers don't quit," perfected placing special operators on targets in the dead of night and on just about any surface imaginable "plus or minus thirty seconds" from the desired time. The unit began as a battalion-sized element known as Task Force 160. Over time, the need for Special Operations aviation grew, and the unit added other battalions and a regimental headquarters. However, the 1st battalion worked alongside some of the best units of the military establishment. To many in the Special Operations community, it remained TF-160, or just Task Force for short.

Night Stalkers served valiantly in numerous missions, from Operation Urgent Fury in Grenada and Just Cause in Panama to Desert Storm in Kuwait. Operation Urgent Fury was Task Force 160th's baptism of fire, only two years after its formation. The occupation of Grenada by Cuban military forces was growing significantly in 1983. In October, the assassination of the communist prime minister and the insertion of an even more Marxist leader, coupled with Cuban workers building an airfield capable of landing military transports, prompted action by the Reagan administration. The medical school located on the island drew approximately one thousand American citizens to Grenada. The initial mission was to be an evacuation of the Americans. President Reagan was committed to preventing another Tehran-style hostage situation. However, at the request of neighboring island governments, the mission was converted from a noncombatant evacuation operation (NEO) to a full-scale invasion and restoration of a legitimate government.[3]

The Special Forces portion of Operation Urgent Fury was known as Task Force 123. TF-123 was given three key missions: execute a helicopter-borne assault on the Richmond Hill Prison, secure the governor general at his mansion, and secure the island's radio transmitter. The first target resulted in the first-ever combat loss for the 160th. While attempting to place elements of the army's elite counterterrorism unit on the prison, intense enemy antiaircraft fire resulted in numerous casualties of the ground force and the death of Captain Keith Lucas, one of the 160th pilots. The mission was aborted and a ground assault was conducted by elements of the U.S. Army's 75th Ranger Regiment.

The assault on the governor's mansion was met with nearly equally intense small arms and antiaircraft fire. The assault element for this operation was a Navy SEAL team. The plan was to insert the first portion of the team by fast rope. The helicopter essentially hovers sixty feet over the target and a large rope is used like a fireman's pole while soldiers jump from the aircraft and slide down the rope onto the target. The SEALs from the first helo were to then cut down trees to allow the second to land. This was necessary because, in addition to the SEALs and SEAL team commander on the second aircraft, there were two Central Intelligence Agency personnel who did not know how to fast rope. Unfortunately, the fire from the enemy was so intense, the tree cutting was canceled, the SEALs on the second aircraft fast roped in, and the Agency boys flew home without getting to the ground. The SEALs quickly took down the target and secured the governor. Soon after, a large force of Cuban military supported by armored personnel carriers assaulted the mansion. The SEALs held the attackers off for twenty-four hours until U.S. Marines reinforced them.[4]

Elements of the SEAL team were again called on for the transmitter mission. An estimated thirteen-hundred Cuban military and two thousand local militia forces were in the vicinity surrounding the transmitter. The 160th flew the insertion, placing the SEALs right on the target with minimal resistance. Within an hour, however, after numerous and heavy enemy counterattacks, the SEALs opted to destroy the transmitter, then escaped and evaded to the coast. They swam to a rendezvous with a Navy destroyer. The Special Operations aspect of Operation Urgent Fury was a success. The Night Stalkers baptism of fire earned them a reputation that resulted in the adoption of the unit's motto, "Night Stalkers don't quit."[5]

Several covert operations from the Middle East to the African continent occurred over the ensuing years. However, the next major test of the Night Stalkers came on orders from President George H.W. Bush (41). In December 1989, the tyrannical dictator of Panama, General Manuel Noriega, assaulted and captured his last American. Newly elected, Bush 41 was convinced it was time to remove the dictator and restore democracy to this strategically critical country. Night Stalkers would play a decisive role.

The vast majority of the missions given to the Special Operations forces for Operation Just Cause were executed in the pre-H-hour assault window. H-hour is the time set for the start of a mission; the special operators were "setting the stage" for a successful assault. Two MH-6 Little Birds inserted the combat controllers, who would in turn beacon the airborne drops of Rangers and 82nd Airborne Division soldiers on their combat parachute assaults of two airfields. Four AH-6 gunship Little Birds used rocket pods to harass the Panamanian Defense Force (PDF) headquarters, located in the Commandancia. During the mission, one of the Little Birds was shot down by heavy enemy small-arms fire, crashing in the center of the Commandancia. After two hours of evasion inside the compound, the unharmed pilots escaped and were later picked up by friendly forces. An additional pre-H-hour mission was a large assault on a beach house located on the Colon Coast of Panama. It was suspected that a large contingent of PDF officers was vacationing at the beach house. During the mission, an AH-6 Little Bird was shot down, with the loss of both pilots. These men were the only Night Stalker fatalities during the operation.[6]

Perhaps the most noteworthy Special Operations mission was the rescue of Kurt Muse. Muse was a U.S. citizen living in Panama who decided to take matters into his own hands. In late 1988, Muse began transmitting anti-Noriega messages throughout the country. The Agency saw an opportunity and equipped Mr. Muse with a very large transmitter, capable of overpowering even Noriega's broadcasts. At the first opportunity, Noriega's PDF captured Muse and placed him in Modelo Prison, a classic Third World confinement facility. Planning for the operation began in earnest well before President Bush's decision for a full invasion. A replica of the prison was built at Eglin Air Force Base and the U.S. Army's elite counterterrorism unit was tasked with the mission.

With AH-6 Little Birds conducting close air support by strafing enemy barracks, and snipers from the army's counterterrorism unit providing surgical guard removal, the assault began. MH-6 Little Birds lifted the counterterrorism unit's operators onto the roof of the prison building Muse was known to occupy. Breach charges opened the roof with a thunderous explosion, initiating the main assault. Operators using night vision goggles moved freely through the prison. Muse was quickly located and moved to the roof to load into the MH-6s. Muse was tucked into the small space behind the pilots of an MH-6 Little Bird, with two operators tucked on both sides. As the aircraft launched off the building, it took heavy enemy fire, causing it to crash to the pavement just outside the prison perimeter. The operators moved Muse to a nearby building and marked their position with infrared strobe lights. Infrared strobes are only visible to people wearing night vision goggles. Night Stalkers identified their location and passed it to an armored infantry unit nearby. The unit picked Muse and the operators up in an M-113 armored personnel carrier, a metal box on tracked wheels, and transported him to Howard Air Force Base. Kurt Muse was a free man.[7]

The Muse rescue was the highlight of the operation and validated the years of preparation for just such a mission. The 1980s had seen several hijackings and hostage takings, beyond the U.S. embassy seizure in Iran. These other missions never produced an opportunity for the operators to demonstrate their capability. The rescue of Kurt Muse was a huge success for the Special Operations community.

However, one mission in Operation Just Cause remained: finding Manuel Noriega. The dictator fled to the safety of the Papal Nuncio, rightly believing the United States would not assault the Catholic church's property. U.S. forces surrounded the facility, and after a few days of negotiations—and some loud rock music blasted from psychological warfare unit's speakers—Noriega surrendered. Two Night Stalker MH-60

Black Hawk's flew the dictator to Howard Air Force Base to begin his long trip to justice.

Desert Storm again demanded the night flying skills of the 160th SOAR pilots and crews. The primary mission was SCUD hunting. Saddam's intention was to use the SCUD missiles to bring Israel into the war in hopes that its involvement would incite Arab States to leave the coalition assembled against him. Using MH-60 Black Hawk helicopters and MH-47 Chinook helicopters, pilots of the 160th SOAR inserted both British Special Air Service (SAS) and the U.S. Army's counterterrorism unit deep into the Iraqi desert. These men essentially roamed the countryside during the war, providing laser-designated target identification for the destruction of SCUD missiles. In direct fire engagements, the 160th SOAR's MH-60L Direct Action Penetrator (DAP) destroyed several SCUDS. The DAP is an armed version of the Black Hawk with impressive twin miniguns that each shoot four thousand rounds of 7.62 mm bullets per minute. A 30 mm cannon and a rocket pod complete the lethal ensemble. It can also be outfitted to fire Hell Fire antitank missiles.

On February 21, 1991, an urgent request for medical evacuation came from one of the army Special Operations teams inside Iraq. One of the operators, while engaged in actions against Iraqi forces, fell from a cliff, severely injuring himself. The 160th SOAR launched an MH-60 for the rescue. After a lengthy and arduous flight only feet above the desert floor, the injured operator plus two teammates were extracted from a pick-up zone in Iraq. As the Night Stalkers and their passengers neared their base of operations, they were caught in a massive sandstorm. The pilots lost all visual reference to the ground and crashed. There were no survivors. These were the only fatalities suffered by the 160th in Desert Storm.

A second rescue mission of a Special Forces operational detachment, the A-Team, was conducted on or about February

24. The team had infiltrated 150 miles inside Iraq, with the mission of observing the Iraqi highways leading south to Kuwait. The commander wanted early warning and details of any enemy reinforcements moving toward Kuwait. The team was compromised when some small children discovered their positions and led family members and Iraqi militia back to the A-Team. The A-Team held off the attackers until night. In the hours of darkness, the Night Stalkers again came to the rescue. The A-Team was found using a beacon device in one of the team member's radios and safely flown to their operating base.[8]

There were other missions no one talks about. Regardless, few people outside of the highly secretive Special Operations Force, or SOF, community were aware of 160th's existence until Operation Gothic Serpent. In August 1993, President Clinton ordered Special Operations forces from the army, along with Task Force 160, to Somalia to capture warlord Mohamed Farrah Aidid, who had stepped up attacks against United Nations forces in an effort to seize primary power in the war-torn country. The operators captured increasingly higher-level lieutenants of Aidid in their initial months in country. In October, a mission designed to capture two senior ranking leaders in Aidid's militia resulted in what many called the most desperate firefight American forces had participated in since Vietnam.

During the battle, two Special Operations helicopters of Task Force 160 were shot down with Russian-made rocket propelled grenade launchers, or RPGs. The firefights surrounding the crews of the downed helicopters lasted well over eighteen hours. The battle resulted in seventy-three wounded. Nineteen Army Rangers, Special Operations aviators, and special operators gave their lives.[9] Approximately seven hundred Somali militia were killed, and estimates of the wounded militia range from one thousand to four thousand. Chief Warrant Officer Michael Durrant, who piloted one of the aircraft, was taken hostage and held for eleven days. His life was saved in part by the actions of two heroic counterterrorism unit operators who volunteered to be inserted to provide protection. Both were posthumously awarded the Medal of Honor. President Clinton subsequently pulled U.S. forces from Somalia, and the incident was tremendously difficult to keep hidden. Subsequent investigations by newspaperman Mark Bowden led to the publication of his book, *Black Hawk Down*. That book was later made into a hugely successful movie by the same name, the creation of which the army and Special Operations community decided to support with pilots, aircraft, and crews from the 160th. The secret black helicopter unit was now public knowledge.

The 160th Special Operations Aviation Regiment I joined had essentially three battalions. Two of these were stationed at Fort Campbell, Kentucky, along with the Regiment's headquarters and supporting units. The medical care for the regiment was provided by a platoon of medics. Each battalion and the regiment had an army physician assigned to it, giving 160th SOAR three doctors in the regiment at Fort Campbell. We provided routine medical care from a single medical clinic located on the unit's compound. The medics all belonged to the regimental physician, and I, as the first battalion doctor, along with the second battalion doctor would be augmented with different medics to do field operations with our respective battalions when deployed for training or combat.

The senior medic at the 160th SOAR, Corey, had served with the 160th for five years by the time I arrived. In that time, and with the assistance of his other medic noncommissioned officers, he had converted the platoon of medics from a primarily "sick call" force to trauma experts. Prior to arriving at the 160th SOAR, Corey had served as a medic in a deep black organization, which often required the services of the 160th when they needed to get from one place to another on the battlefield. During that time he realized that while the shooter on the ground had a medic with him trained in trauma stabilization, once the patient was placed on the aircraft, there was no one trained to do patient care in the aircraft. Oftentimes these patients suffered while enduring a lengthy flight back to a medical team. In his time in that covert unit, he developed a vision for what the 160th medics could become: the providers during flight. At the first opportunity to move to the 160th, he took the job and the challenge.

When he arrived at the 160th, the medics of the unit never flew missions with the pilots. They were primarily trained to treat minor ailments, handing out Motrin and the occasional antibiotic. Corey made it his life's work to see that change. Over the course of years, he was able to reverse a mentality at the regiment's headquarters. However, it would take combat to change the minds of all the players in the Special Operations world.

For obvious reasons, Special Operations planners want to maximize the number of shooters on the target. When the shooters are several hours away from their base of operations and have several mountain ranges between the target and the launch point, they only get to dance with the ones they bring with them. The pilots calculate fuel and weights based on temperatures and altitudes and then tell the shooters how many people they can load on each aircraft. What ultimately happens is a fight to get every man on the birds for the mission. When the 160th SOAR customer, be it a Navy SEAL team or whomever, hears the number, they invariably want more. This sets up a dynamic where the 160th leadership is torn. Do we put our medics in the flight and thus decrease the number of shooters by one or two? Are we handicapping this commando's ability to do his mission? Of course, the shooter always says that he has his own medical people who will make the flight back and who can care for the wounded en route. Up until 9-11, the ground guys almost always won the argument.

September 11, 2001, began as any other fall day in America and ended with Special Operations forces beginning mission analysis and deployment planning. The initial Special Operations forces used in the effort to unseat the Taliban were split into two task forces. One based itself in Uzbekistan, flying missions in from the north; the other was based on an aircraft carrier in the Arabian Sea. In time, as most of the Taliban and Al Qaeda were swept away, these forces converged at Bagram, Afghanistan. Bagram offered a Russian-built airfield capable of landing all the necessary support aircraft. It was rumored to be the site where Alexander the Great died from illness at the end of his great campaigns. The United States Special Operations command would now use it as a major base of operations in the hunt for Bin Laden.

By February 2002, the Taliban and Al-Qaeda fighters, joined by jihadists from all over the Arab world, had consolidated in the mountainous regions of the Paktika Province. An elaborate network of caves discovered and capitalized on years before by the mujahedeen as they fought the Russian invader of the 1980s hid them and significant caches of weapons. Interception of enemy electronic transmissions via phone, cell phone, and two-way radio had numerous intelligence analysts believing that America's most wanted, Osama Bin Laden, was present in the province. Most of the enemy was believed to occupy an area known as the Shah-e-Kot valley, just southeast of Gardez, Afghanistan, and the surrounding mountains.

In February 2002, Major General Hagenbeck, commander of the U.S. Army's major forces in the area, devised a classic "hammer and anvil" maneuver code named Operation Anaconda.[10] The hammer, comprised of primarily Afghan fighters, was led by militia leader Zia Lodin and directed by two Special Forces operational detachment teams. They were to drive into the area where the enemy forces were holed up. The hope was that the enemy would then flee to the east toward

Pakistan.[11] Placed along various egress routes would be the soldiers of the 101st Airborne Division and the 10th Mountain Division, welcomingly serving as the anvil. Unites States Special Operations forces of all branches of the service, joined by spec ops units from several other coalition countries, were placed at strategic points throughout the area to provide reconnaissance of enemy movements.

As the battle unfolded, the enemy halted the movement of Task Force Hammer as they stood and fought instead of fleeing. To the east and south, enemy forces began aggressive attacks against the Task Force Anvil forces. In one particular area, known as Landing Zone (LZ) Ginger, the attacks were severe, and the need to place additional Special Operations reconnaissance teams near the LZ led Hagenbeck to get "eyes on" the enemy movements in and around the U.S. and Afghani forces there.

On March 2, 2002, the command sent two Navy SEAL teams to Takur Ghar, a ten thousand–foot snow-capped peak with commanding views of the various areas of operation. Flying them were two Special Operations MH-47s of the 160th SOAR. Razor 03 and Razor 04, the radio call signs of the two birds ferrying the soldiers, launched at 1 AM. Around 0300 hours, or 3 AM, and significantly later than planned, Razor 03 approached its landing zone, a small saddle on the top of Takur Ghar. As the aircraft began its flare just prior to touch down, it came under withering small arms and machine gun fire. It is believed an RPG hit the helo somewhere near the tail ramp where the SEAL team was standing, waiting to hop onto the mountain. The damage to the aircraft prevented any lift from the rotors. In what to most would seem an insane act, the pilot, instead of completing the touch down, pushed the controls and essentially dropped the helo off the backside of the mountain. As it fell, wind created spin in the blades, which provided enough lift to prevent a crash. This amazing feat of flying saved the crew and passengers, except one. As the men conducted a head count, the SEALs realized they were short one man. Navy SEAL Petty Officer Neal Roberts had fallen off the ramp on top of the mountain.[12]

Razor 04 landed with Razor 03, collected the Navy SEALs and downed crewman and then flew back to Gardez. An Air Force C-130 Specter Gunship monitoring the hilltop reported seeing what they thought was Petty Officer Roberts. The remaining SEALs formulated a plan and then pleaded with the Special Operations pilots on Razor 04. In the Special Operations community, "leave no man behind" is a religious obligation. The pilots and crew were eager to help. At 0500 local time, the four remaining members of Robert's SEAL team, accompanied by Air Force Combat Controller John Chapman, were placed back into the landing lone (LZ) atop Takur Ghar. As the five men moved forward, they were engaged by Taliban and Al Qaeda forces dug in on the hilltop. In only a matter of minutes, Chapman was killed and two of the Navy SEALs were wounded. They recognized they were against impossible odds, and not finding Roberts, the men broke contact and moved off the mountaintop. As they withdrew, they radioed their higher headquarters, requesting them to launch the Quick Reaction Force (QRF).[13]

A QRF of army Rangers and other Special Operations forces, whose mission was to standby as a reserve force to be committed at a moment's notice, was launched just before sunrise. Razor 01 and Razor 02, each an MH-47 from 160th SOAR, arrived at the target area just as daylight made the Night Stalker's night vision goggles useless. They were directed to a different LZ, but in the confusion created by communications problems, they landed in essentially the same spot as Razor 03 and Razor 04. Limited information reached the QRF leader, Ranger Lieutenant Self. The QRF proceeded into the LZ with little knowledge that there was a large Al Qaeda force dug in with interlocking machine gun positions set at close range to cover the LZ.

On the final approach, Corey, the 160th SOAR's senior medic and the medic on Razor 01, was asked by the door gunner to step away from him. As Corey moved down the fuselage of the MH-47, gunfire erupted from the sides, and RPGs streaked from multiple directions. One was believed to have flown through the aircraft lengthwise. The aircraft was immediately out of commission, unable to fly even had the pilots been well enough to do so. Corey was knocked down by at least two bullets, which struck the visor of his flight helmet. He woke up with blood streaming into his eyes as bullets continued to turn the fuselage of the MH-47 into Swiss cheese. The fuel tanks on the sides of the Chinook are made of Kevlar armor coating. For the time being, they were providing some protection.

Corey immediately began triaging a patient in his vicinity. He first realized that the door gunner, who had asked him to step away, probably saved his life. The gunner's lifeless body lay just near where Corey had been standing. Shortly after realizing the door gunner was dead, an RPG exploded in the cockpit, throwing one of the pilots back into the main passenger compartment and right in front of Corey. The pilot had an arterial bleed that was quickly spurting his blood all over the back of the aircraft. Corey withdrew his old-school tourniquet pack and placed a tourniquet on the artery. Over the ensuing hours of the fight, Corey would return to the wounded pilot, release the tourniquet to allow blood to revitalize the tissue and then replace it. This act, while unconventional, probably saved the pilot's hand.[14]

As Corey completed his bandaging of the pilot, another crewmember noticed a fire that had started between the pilot's area and the rear cargo area. One of the rear door gunners tossed Corey an extinguisher. However, as he jumped up to spray the fire, a bullet slammed into the back plate of his body armor, pounding him back into the floor of the helo. Fortunately for everyone, the burst from his extinguisher did its job. Corey was soon called to the back ramp, where just outside the helo, the other Night Stalker pilot laid.[15] Someone had placed a tourniquet on the pilot's thigh and wanted Corey's assessment. Meanwhile, the Rangers outside the aircraft had already taken three KIAs and were, for the time being, unable to do anything more than suppress enemy fire. Over the course of the next two and a half hours, Corey, along with an air force pararescue jumper, or PJ, attended the many wounded and consolidated them in a small depression at the back of the MH-47.[16]

Around 0830 hours, the remainder of the QRF aboard Razor 02, which at the moment Razor 01 crashed into the LZ was directed to return to Gardez, touched down in an alternate LZ two thousand feet below the peak. Over the next two hours, these men moved up a 75 percent slope, with three feet of snow, carrying weapons, ammunition, body armor, and other implements of war. Once on the hill, they linked up with the six rangers from Razor 01 and conducted an assault on the enemy positions. In a matter of minutes, the Rangers were conducting mop ups, clearing out the remaining terrorists and consolidating ammunition and supplies.[17] The Ranger lieutenant had Corey and the air force PJ move the casualty collection point to the top of the hill as he and his Rangers set up a defensive perimeter. As the men stood for the first time and grabbed litters loaded with wounded comrades, enemy small-arms fire struck hard and furious from another peak four hundred meters to the rear of the downed helo. The wounded at the casualty collection point were in the open and pinned down, as were Corey and the PJ attending them.

Exposing themselves to the enemy fire, Corey and the PJ continued to move the patients, making at least three trips in the open. Soon after the engagement began, both Cory and the PJ were hit by a burst from an enemy AK-47. Both were struck in the abdomen. The PJ's wounds included a liver laceration, a wound that bleeds profusely, with little ability to apply pressure and staunch blood flow.[18] The bullets hitting Corey pierced his bladder. As he lay clutching the wound, a fourth round smacked his buttocks. The medic assigned to the Rangers took over the care of the wounded. Exposing themselves to continuous enemy fire, the Rangers and remaining Night Stalker crewmembers moved the wounded to a covered and concealed position. Inside the defensive perimeter, Corey the medic was now the patient. However, despite his many wounds, Corey continued to direct the young Ranger medic and other Rangers and Night Stalkers on the hill in the care of the other patients. As the day ebbed into night, he resolved he would not die on that hill. Just before sunset, the PJ, named Jason, succumbed to his wounds.[19]

At about 2015 local time, four SOAR MH-47s extracted the force, all wounded and all dead, which included Petty Officer Roberts and the Air Force Controller John Chapman. A forward surgical team stationed in the air traffic control tower of Bagram Airport surgically stabilized the wounded. Later the following day, they were flown to hospitals in Germany and then on to Walter Reed Army Medical Center in Washington, D.C.[20]

Corey's actions on the hill that day earned him a Silver Star. More importantly to Corey, it earned him and his medics an irreplaceable reputation as the best combat medics in the army. The PJ was awarded the Air Force Cross for valor in combat. The Air Force Cross is second only to the Congressional Medal of Honor. By the time I signed in to 160th SOAR, Corey had been home for four months and was back in charge, leading the medical platoon and serving the soldiers and aviators of the unit. He would not have to wait long to climb aboard another MH-47 headed into combat against the nation's enemies. Just imagine that … after being shot approximately seven times, in less than a year, he would climb back into an aircraft and launch on the opening missions of Operation Iraqi Freedom. The bravery of this man, and the medics whom he led, was unparalleled.

Chapter Four

The Hunt for the Smoking Gun

In the buildup to invade Iraq, senior U.S. leaders wanted to find a smoking gun. While the reasons to oust Saddam Hussein were many, everyone wanted to prove he possessed weapons of mass destruction and, better yet, a link with Al Qaeda. In early December 2002, only a few months after arriving at the 160th, I was walking through the flight line of one of the aircraft hangars when a platoon medic found me and said the battalion operations officer was looking for me. The medic seemed unusually anxious, and his energy quickly transferred to me. In a Special Operations unit with the mission to deploy at a moment's notice, it takes very little to spin the new guy up. I ran to the ops officer's planning area, sucking in lungfuls of air and knowing full well he must have been smirking at my rookie exuberance.

The operations officer, Mark, was the typical Special Operations pilot. He had spent multiple tours with the unit as a Black Hawk pilot, even commanding one of the unit's assault companies. Mark was one laid-back guy; very little got his blood pressure up. While I was perspiring with a heart rate well over one hundred beats per minute, he was quite calm and motioned me to a map on his desk. "Doc, we've got a mission that stands a good chance of going off." He then oriented me to a map of Iraq. It seemed that in the northeastern region of Iraq, an agency source had collected a chemical vial sample from what was believed to be an Al Qaeda training facility. The area was extremely close to the border with Iran and was north of the No Fly Zone, out of Saddam's influence. The vial tested positive for cyanide. Mark told me to pack my gear for a three-day planning mission.

Later that week, I deployed with Kevin, a senior SOAR medic, to a very remote and highly classified planning facility on one of our nation's military bases. The facility is hidden in the middle of a training area, surrounded by forests and a very secure series of fences. It was patrolled constantly, even when no one was occupying the planning areas. Kevin and I reported to the gate, and our special badges got us through the series of checkpoints. Mark had instructed us to find a bunk in the barracks and then report to the planning cell.

This was my first exposure both to the people with whom I would conduct many Special Operations missions and to their methods. I was joining people who had worked together for many years. Most had already planned numerous combat missions in Afghanistan and other places around the word. My Ranger tab and other infantry badges bought me some credibility. But you only have to spend a day in the army to know there are soldiers with lots of badges whom you would not want on your team—and several who failed to get the tabs and badges but whom you would pay to have in the foxhole next to you. I wanted to ensure my medics, and I got to go on the mission. That meant meeting as many key people as possible and assisting them where allowed. Kevin and I moved through the planning meetings, introducing ourselves first to the ground team that would do the assault and then all the medical players vying to be a part of this historic and extremely classified mission.

One of the interesting points about the early stages of the War on Terror was that everyone wanted to be involved. There were numerous turf battles fought for every mission. In the past, determining which medics flew on the mission often depended on who was doing the mission. Army Special Operations units always carried their own medics with them, so when there was limited room on the assault aircraft, the aviation unit flying them would frequently back down and not insist on SOAR medics joining the operation. That changed with Robert's Ridge. Corey's actions had won a great deal of respect for not only himself but the entire SOAR medical platoon. The Night Stalker pilots were insistent that at least one SOAR medic fly in the flight. However, with air force pararescue, numerous army Special Operations medical personnel, army ground medical personnel, SOAR medics, and myself, the SOAR flight surgeon, the battle still needed to be fought to ensure we got to go to this party.

The Special Operations commander who was running the ground portion of this operation was a hulk of a man. Mark McGwire, the barrel chested home run king, had nothing on this guy. "Jim" had been with his organization for many years, and his noncommissioned officers treated him with reverence. In the Special Operations community, the senior enlisted men often planned and led the operations. Jim did most of the talking. He was about my age, and while we did not know one another, we had been infantry officers together. I presented my rationale for letting Kevin and me fly with his men on the mission.

Our helicopters would be the primary means for conveying his shooters to the target. He, of course, wanted his medics to fly in the formation so they would be available for the initial assessment of patients on the ground. His medical people would do an initial stabilization and get the patients onto our aircraft. One of the aircraft flying in this type of formation was always designated the primary casualty evacuation or CASEVAC, while another was secondary. Who did the medical care inside the aircraft was still being negotiated by the time I arrived at the Special Operations community.

My role was to ensure that the best medical personnel for the mission were in the aircraft. Our medics and doctors trained on the 160th aircraft daily. The pilots and crews were our people; we lived and worked as members of the same unit. We placed the equipment in the helos and trained on it continuously. We knew we were the best medical team for the care of the patient once the patient got into the aircraft. It became my mission to convince the others of these facts. To do so, I chose to speak the language I knew from having been a prior infantry officer. Whenever an operator goes to plan a mission, he first looks at the situation. From their earliest training, young infantryman and other army warriors are taught the acronym METT-T (pronounced "met tea"), which reminds them of the various aspects of the situation. M stands for mission, E for enemy forces, and the Ts for time, terrain, and troops available. Our mission would be to handle any casualty, keep him alive up to what in civilian medical terms would be called definitive care, or someone who can fix what's broken. For most missions, that meant a surgeon. For this mission, it meant both a surgeon and a physician who could treat the effects of cyanide poisoning.

The enemies to the medical planner are the weapons available to the bad guys and the types of wounds those weapons create. Planning has to take into account all the possible wounds the enemy is equipped and trained to inflict. Predicting the wounds drives the resources stocked in the aircraft needed to assess and stabilize the patient. Time in medical terms was simply reduced to, "How long do I have to keep the wounded alive in the back of a blacked out Special Operations helicopter?" Spec Ops aviators tend to hate medics and docs who whip out white light to assess patients. Besides "whiting out" their night vision goggles (NVGs), it tends to paint a nice target for the bad guys looking for an Al Jazeera video clip. We molded the terrain assessment to mean what kind of flight and the type aircraft on which we would be flying.

Working on a patient in the back of a MH-60K Black Hawk was significantly more cumbersome than working in the back of a MH-47E Chinook, unless of course the "hook" had sixty plus Navy SEALs jammed into the back of it. Again, all of these specifics are considered in the METT-T analysis.

This mission was a significant challenge for the medical planners for two reasons. The flight was extremely long. Our intermediate staging base (ISB) was located in a friendly country, but the target was deep in Iraq, right on the Iraq-Iran border. Definitive care, the surgeons and advanced critical care physicians and team members, were staying in the ISB. That meant any wounded soldier, whether by blast, bullets, or chemical weapons, needed to be stabilized for a two-hour flight, again in the back of the blacked out helicopters.

The trauma piece was the easier part. Treating trauma is essentially an algorithm. By traditional algorithms, stabilizing trauma victims involves first protecting their ability to breath or breathing for them. Secondly, we simultaneously stop bleeding and replace the lost volume of blood. There are other tasks, such as stabilizing fractures and assessing the chest wall for function, however the initial field evaluation has to get the patient breathing and blood loss stymied. The equipment to do this is fairly simple. We could intubate patients (place a tube in their airway and breathe for them) if we had to. We could start IVs and give different types of fluids based on the patient's needs and the amount of blood loss. We could relieve any chest wall injury that might either constrict breath or result in a loss of pressure in the lung cavity and thus the ability to pull air into the lungs. Treating trauma is typically just a walk down the algorithm, down the A, B, Cs. Picture most any trauma scene in the old TV show *ER* and you have it. Except that it happens in a seven-foot by eight-foot space in a helo crammed full of people and equipment. Pitch black. Enemy fire. 170 MPH. To people you know.

The difficulty with this mission revolved around the cyanide. Army medics are some of the best-trained trauma stabilizers in the world. Special Operations medics are even better. However, the degree of internal medicine, or advanced critical care medical management, these fine soldiers receive is lacking due to the nature of their training. The metabolic derangements produced by chemical weapons require constant monitoring and subtle manipulations with medicines and fluids. These are medical decisions that are best treated by a person trained in toxicology.

Cyanide disrupts how the body produces energy by binding to a certain enzyme, or chemical machinery, in the cells of our bodies. It essentially converts all the body's cells into a sprint like state. When a person sprints, they switch from aerobic (lots of oxygen present) to anaerobic metabolism (very little oxygen available). When deprived of oxygen, our muscles use alternatives, which leads to a build-up of certain acids in the tissues. This causes the burning sensation a sprinter gets near the end of a sprint. As the situation continues, the tissues are unable to produce energy and their vital functions cease. A cascade of events occurs, leading to the death of the tissue. Cyanide blocks the body's ability to function aerobically, thus producing an oxygen-deprived state inside nearly every single cell in the body. Every cell and tissue builds up lactic acid, creating the effects that ultimately lead to death. The initial symptoms include headache, light-headedness, balance disturbances, excitement, anxiety, a burning sensation, increased heart rate, and high blood pressure. Eventually, patients slip into a coma, begin to have seizures, develop fluid on their lungs, and have palpitations and heart failure. Cyanide poisoning can be reversed in the early stages, but when these later symptoms begin, it takes immediate attention and a Herculean effort to save the patient's life.

The treatment for cyanide poisoning is complex. Patients can breath the chemical antidote or get it through an IV;

typically, both methods are used. The inhaled version, amyl nitrate, is believed to begin work almost immediately. These antidotes form a complex in the patient's bloodstream, which causes the cyanide to bind to it instead of the enzyme where it wreaks havoc. Now that the cyanide is no longer disrupting the cell's enzymes, there is time for another antidote to do its job. The second antidote is also given through the IV, where it then binds to cyanide to form a nontoxic chemical the body urinates away. So essentially, physicians treating cyanide poisoning need to be able to give an inhaled drug and two IV drugs. For us, that means an inhaled drug and two IV drugs in the back of a blacked out Special Operations helo, crammed full of shooters and their combat equipment, evading an enemy we just assaulted, deep in Iraq and on the Iranian border.

The aviation "package," a term used to encompass all aircraft, crews, and the customers on board for the flight to the target, would be large and would require both a primary and a secondary CASEVAC platform. Because of the potential chemical weapons, the number of possible patients could be extremely large as well. In fact, if the entire target was saturated with cyanide, potentially all the shooters and aviators could be casualties. Even with two aircraft staffed with medical personnel, the demand for medical resources could easily exceed the supply. Further, because chemical weapons often do not produce immediate symptoms, a shooter could climb aboard a nonmedical platform for return and develop symptoms on the return flight. Stopping along the route home, after hitting an enemy target hundreds of miles inside Iraq and near the Iranian border, would be less than ideal. Consequently, we needed to place cyanide antidote on every aircraft and develop a means for the shooters to treat themselves. Remember, that's an inhaled drug and two IV drugs, in a cramped helo, pitch black …

The plan Kevin and I came up with was a joint effort. Kevin was a meticulous logistician. He was an introvert, extremely quiet unless there were a few beers on board. Kevin had a lovely wife and two boys. My first social gathering with the unit was a party at his house. It was great to see him loosen up about midway through the keg. He had a heart of gold, and no one, not even Corey, had more commitment to the 160th SOAR than Kevin. But his greatest asset was an unfathomable need for perfection. I would never say Kevin was clinically obsessive compulsive, but he was extremely meticulous. It served him and the medical platoon of the 160th SOAR well. Kevin was the platoon's logistician. He traced every item in the unit's inventory, packaged all the medical sets and kits for combat and training, and made sure soldiers deploying had all the gear they needed to include their medical equipment. Kevin could recite exactly how many cyanide antidote kits were on hand, incomplete, and on order. Kevin had supernatural ability when it came to tracking parts and supplies. He was a unique and talented guy.

Knowing the exact number of antidote kits on hand, and all the supporting equipment needed to administer them, made him essential to developing the plan for this operation. We had enough of the inhaled drug to give each soldier two ampules. The plan we came up with was to have the soldiers tape the drug inside their chemical protective mask. The drug is similar to smelling salts; you have to break it in order to release the drug. If anyone felt they were getting early symptoms, they were to notify a buddy, who would break the vial so the patient inhaled the drug inside their mask. All 160th aviators and all the operators were trained to start IVs and would do so once the amyl nitrate vials were broken and activated. The medications, both IV antidotes, were premixed, one per shooter and aviator in each bird. The bags would be numbered with luminescent ink. The shooter would then hang the bag of antidotes in numbered order and allow them to go into his friend via the IV. Considering the constraints, we felt the plan was acceptable.

We briefed the ground commander, letting him know that we knew the airframes better than anyone, since we were directly assigned to the 160th, which was flying his shooters to the target. The medical equipment was placed by us, planned by us, and maintained by us. Of course I mentioned the success of our medics at en route stabilization of patients in the War on Terror to date. It was the first time I had used the term "en route stabilization," and it seemed to connect with the ground commander for this operation. I defined it to the commander by referencing the death of Princess Diana and the differences between ambulance practices in Europe and the United States. In America, our paramedics do as little as they have to at the scene and do most of their work on the patient en route to definitive care. Our philosophy holds that the key to saving the most people from trauma is getting the patient to the hospital definitive care as quickly as possible. This technique is often described as a "scoop and run." It was speculated that Princess Di's chances for survival would have been significantly greater had the paramedics initiated transport sooner. My understanding was she had a torn aorta, which can only be repaired surgically in an operating room. In Europe, the thinking is to do as much stabilization in the field. In this particular injury, any delay is significant. From then on the term "en route stabilization," referring to the care provided in the helicopter, stuck. For every future mission I planned in the unit, our medics were briefed as the "troops available" — again playing on the ground commander's METT-T mindset — for "en route stabilization." With Corey and the other medic's success in OEF, and this term and corresponding concept, the ground commanders seemed to understand, and the battle to get 160th SOAR medics on the flights got easier and easier.

After three days of planning, the real world hit: it was time to practice. The operators and aviators planned a hit on an abandoned chemical plant near the army post where we conducted the planning. Due to bad weather, the aviation piece of the practice was canceled. The shooters, however, still wanted to practice their "actions on the objective." But they needed a "backside" medical resource. Whenever a training mission was conducted, the medical plan had to include treating, both pretend casualties and real-world injuries. When these men trained, they did so at full speed. This often meant real-world casualties such as broken legs from falling through an obstacle. When this happened, the unit conducting the training would not want to stop the training exercise, wasting the money and time spent to organize the training. Further, they would not want to interrupt the medical people currently part of the training exercise. Therefore, a redundant medical team was always present for the real-world injuries. This backside medical piece typically stayed out of the way of the training scenario, but was available immediately should a shooter be injured. Kevin and I were honored when the ground commander asked us to go on the target with his men and serve as their backside medical team. It was a compliment for both of us and the 160th SOAR medics, and it further enhanced a relationship with this particular special ops ground unit that would further pave the way for unparalleled opportunities to serve them during the War on Terror.

We returned to our home base with a solid plan should the president of the United States (POTUS) authorize the mission. Ultimately, the mission was scratched. We believed POTUS had made the decision to launch the full-scale invasion, and with the intel we had on other targets, most leaders assumed there would be plenty of opportunities to identify the WMD smoking gun. This supposed training facility for Al Qaeda became a cruise missile target in the shock and awe phase of Operation Iraqi Freedom. For the time being, I would have to wait. Panama, Desert Storm/Shield, Somalia, and now what would have been an historic flight and operation were creating a trend of missed opportunities for me. Frustration at what I thought was bad luck was mounting.

Chapter Five

Combat Preparations

Even before the operation to find the source of the cyanide vial, planning was in the works for the invasion of Iraq. The Special Operations aviation package was being calculated aggressively, based on the missions the higher Special Operations command was giving the 160th SOAR. In a broad sense, medical personnel exist to sustain the fighting force by returning wounded soldiers to the action. We also serve to create confidence in the fighting force. It has been proven that where soldiers and aviators believe their medical team will keep them alive if wounded, those soldiers fight more tenaciously and confidently. The quality of the medical team means a more motivated fighting force. Every medic understands this. Further, the men flying the missions were our friends. All the medical personnel were committed to ensuring that no man failed to come home because we were not ready.

Our first planning missions detailed the type and scope of the missions we felt the Task Force would be asked to perform. Corey, along with Andy, the regimental flight surgeon, and the other senior medic leaders knew more than I about how the various packages of aircraft would be broken down during the actual operations. So far, I had only conducted four Special Operations training missions with the unit. They were the experts on how many aircraft would traditionally be used for which type of Special Operations mission. Having worked with our customers, the special operators, for years they knew well the packages the customers would request for each specific mission set. Since my battalion, 1st Battalion, 160th, would be the lead agent for Special Operations aviation support during OIF, I brought the mission sets from the battalion's operational planning to them. They could then more accurately determine the medical package loads.

Corey and the medics had worked for years to configure the equipment in the aircraft for trauma. Each Special Operations airframe rigged for MEDEVAC had a set pattern and package location for every piece of medical equipment. Unique hanging bags had compartments from top to bottom. Any medic who climbed on a 160th SOAR helicopter knew right where to go for things as specific as flutter value bandages designed for sucking chest wounds. The kits included bandages, tourniquets, and all sorts of tools for stopping blood flow. There were also handy packets for establishing intravenous lines, or IVs. The various pieces were placed into a plastic bag and sealed with a food sealer. When you grabbed a 160th SOAR IV kit, you knew what was in it, in order, as you went through the kit. This degree of consistency was critical. Unlike in the back of an ambulance in Miami or on the gurney in your local ER, these SOAR medics did what they did in the dark of night, in the back of a helicopter flying evasive maneuvers, most often filled with shooters, each sucking lungfuls of air as they jumped back on the choppers after assaulting an enemy target. In a time like that, you do not want to be looking for your trauma sheers.

When the kits were loaded, there was always a set place for them in each type of helicopter. In addition to the kits, there were oxygen bottles and cardiovascular monitors that continuously measured heart rate, blood pressure, and the oxygen saturation, meaning a rough measure of the amount of oxygen in the blood stream. There was also a portable, battery-operated suction device. In essence, it produced suction to remove debris and blood from the mouth of a patient the medic needed to intubate. Corey, Kevin, and the other medics had included splint kits for broken bones. There were also specially modified litters for hoisting patients should the area be too small for the helicopter to land for pickup. It was quite an impressive set-up, and one that had already been vetted in combat in Afghanistan.

The curve ball in the build-up for Operation Iraqi Freedom was the weapons of mass destruction. We knew Hussein once had a large supply of nerve and mustard gas, both of which are extremely lethal. Acquiring equipment and medications to treat chemical patients took painstaking planning.

Prior to actually purchasing equipment, the medical logisticians needed a true METT-T assessment of Saddam's capabilities. As Sun Tzu, an ancient Chinese general, said,

> So it is said that if you know your enemies and know yourself, you will fight without danger in battles. If you only know yourself, but not your opponent, you may win or may lose. If you know neither yourself nor your enemy, you will always endanger yourself.[1]

Many of today's military leaders interpret this passage differently. However, clearly knowing your enemy is critical to success. It is also possible that your enemy may have read Sun Tzu, so if you want to win, know your enemy better than he knows you. Unfortunately, Saddam was a master of one of Sun Tzu's other dictums of warfare: "All warfare is based on deception."[2] Few really knew what Saddam's chemical, biologic, and nuclear capabilities were.

U.S. intelligence forces were keenly aware of Saddam's use of both mustard gas and nerve agents in his murderous campaigns against the nationalistic Kurds and the Iranians during the Iran-Iraq War, which lasted from September 1980 to August 1988. Recent intelligence regarding the discovery of the cyanide vial clearly placed that agent on the list of potential enemy weapons. Saddam's association with the Soviet Union created the need to ensure we covered for any possible technology transfers or even actual weapons transfers. For years, U.S. Army leaders were aware the Soviets had weaponized small pox. Small pox is an extremely deadly virus that was eradicated through an aggressive vaccination program. The last reported case of small pox was in Kenya in February 1977. Essentially, there is no small pox in the world today because of this vaccination campaign. Unfortunately, immunization lasts only ten years, making nearly everyone on the planet now susceptible to this virus, which kills one third, or more than 30 percent of the people who get the illness. Further, it is highly contagious. Once released, it would spread rapidly to bystanders. An outbreak occurred in 1971 of a very virulent experimental strain accidentally released into the air during a Soviet field test. Seven vaccinated individuals were made sick by this genetically enhanced version of the virus.[3] What we did not know was that a Soviet virologist, Neja Maltseva, who worked at the Research Institute for Viral Preparations in Moscow until her death in 2000, apparently traveled multiple times to Iraq in the years prior to her death. The *New York Times* published an article on her trips to Iraq about the time we read the intelligence reports in preparation for the operation. Army Intelligence added small pox to the list of potential weapons of mass destruction in the Hussein arsenal.[4]

The Soviet Union had other chemical and biological weapons at its disposal. With the possibility that small pox strains may have been given to Hussein, we had to consider the lesser suspects of anthrax and ricin. The Soviets had an accidental release of anthrax in 1979 from a production plant in Sverdlovsk. Of the one hundred people affected, seventy died. Additionally, the biologic toxin derived from castor beans, ricin, was known to be in the Soviet arsenal.[5] Allegedly, a Soviet dissident was assassinated with ricin in 1978. With Soviet WMD scientists traveling freely to and from Iraq, it was only prudent to prepare for all of these agents. Unfortunately, all of these agents, including small pox, paled in significance to the even minute possibility that Saddam might have a nuclear capability.

Gen. Hussein Kamel, the former director of Iraq's weapons program, defected to Jordan in August 1995, together with his brother Col. Saddam Kamel. Hussein Kamel took crates of documents revealing past weapons programs, and he provided these to UNSCOM. Kamel stated, "I made the decision to disclose everything so that Iraq could return to normal."[6] Iraq responded by revealing a major store of documents that showed that Iraq had begun an unsuccessful crash program to develop a nuclear bomb (on August 20, 1995). After granting several interviews, Hussein and Saddam Kamel agreed to return to Iraq, where they were assassinated on February 23, 1996. Before his return to Iraq and subsequent execution, Kamel did state that Iraq destroyed its nuclear program after the first Gulf War. However his defection and subsequent death began an aggressive intelligence search to determine exactly Saddam's nuclear capability.[7]

As we went to war, senior intelligence personnel felt Hussein probably had not yet acquired fissile material, but they were certain he was trying to do so. They acknowledged there was no way to be certain Hussein had not acquired enough for a single bomb. In President George W. Bush's (43) State of the Union Address, he uttered the sentence, "The British government has learned that Saddam Hussein recently sought significant quantities of uranium from Africa."[8] At the time President Bush made the comment, all the major intelligence services—Britain, the United States and the Soviet Union—were in agreement over a trip made to Niger in 1999 by Hussein officials.[9] A CIA analyst sent her husband on an unpaid fact-finding trip, which resulted in the Nigerians denying the claim. In July 2003, her husband, Joseph Wilson, announced that the Iraqi visitors to Niger were not there to acquire fissile material.[10] This analysis resulted in significant doubt for many people in the United States and Europe. Accusations were levied against the president for intentionally misleading the American people. However a formal commission in Britain called the Butler Commission and a U.S. Senate bipartisan investigation concluded that it was reasonable for the intelligence community to conclude Hussein was attempting to buy fissile uranium ore.[11] Regardless of the various accusations, most people with a minimal amount of awareness of Hussein's megalomaniacal style concluded he sought every type of weapon he could get to achieve regional hegemony. Ultimately, when you are preparing to go to war, it takes very little evidence to convince you of a need to be trained for every contingency. Regardless of the political debate, we had a responsibility and the internal motivation to train for chemical, nuclear, and biologic threats. Call it a survival instinct.

We also could not forget the less glamorous portion of our responsibilities as medical leaders: preventive medicine. Since the dawn of warfare, disease had traditionally been the largest casualty producer on the battlefield. Throughout history, entire armies were incapacitated by dysentery and other such camp pathogens. The army classifies all noncombat action deaths as "disease/non-battle" (DNB). During the Civil War, there were 140,414 combat related deaths compared to 224,097 DNB deaths. With the development of antibiotics, the number of U.S. DNB losses during all of World War II fell to 113,842.[12] The deaths are significant, but even temporary illness among a small, specialized aviation unit could significantly impact the unit's ability to conduct its specific missions. With only one unit in the military capable of flying the missions assigned to the army's Night Stalkers, we knew that any infectious disease running rampant in our camp could significantly affect the entire Special Operation task force's mission. Imagine half the flight crews incapacitated by a gastronomical illness with constant vomiting and diarrhea. It would be a little hard to fly precision aircraft missions in combat. We resolved to not take a single DNB casualty.

The plan to equip, train up, and deploy came together over a few weeks. Since the official word of a decision by the president had not been given, the plan was called a CONPLAN or contingency plan. Once President Bush made it official, CONPLAN 1003 became OPPLAN (operational plan) 1003. The name change meant little to us. We knew all along it was coming, and our intensity level was already pegged in the red.

In addition to training ourselves, the medical leaders of the regiment desired to augment the medical training of every aviator deploying to the fight. In the initial training of all 160th SOAR personnel, each aviator and crewmember was trained on how to stop bleeding and start IVs. Corey and the medical noncommissioned officer leaders coordinated additional combat medical training for all the soldiers. IV and hemorrhage control skills were refreshed. I gave lectures to all the aviators on the effects and treatment of nerve agents as well as other chemical and biological weapons. The soldiers would each carry nerve agent antidote kits and need to fully understand when and how to use these spring-loaded needle devices designed to inject the antidote into the thigh. I had the aviators in my class push the auto injector into oranges so they could feel the violence of the auto-injection and see the needle afterward. Knowledge in a situation like that creates confidence. Again, my job as a medical officer was to create confidence in the fighting force.

Further, our medical personnel had to prepare the "medical kits" for each soldier who deployed. Corey and the guys spent many late nights preparing first aid packs for every soldier. Each of the three hundred men who deployed with the task force, had a bag of IV fluids, various bandages, a tourniquet, IV starter kits, nerve agent antidotes, and once in country, each man was given a morphine auto injector for pain control. Coordinating the medical supplies for the kits alone was daunting, and assembling them was equally time-consuming.

The medics sacrificed a lot of their personal time prior to leaving their families to ready the men for combat. It takes commitment to sacrifice family time when those moments may well be the last you ever spend with them. A father looks at his son, knowing he is leaving for war in only a few weeks. The thought that these last few days are all he may have for his son's lifetime of memories haunts the soldier as he prepares for battle. Time is what you have; it is all you have. Spending it readying for war increases the chance of survival and return. But it also robs the soldier and his family of the last few moments prior to deployment. That last trip for an ice cream cone with your daughter in hopes of creating memories of her dad is extremely difficult to sacrifice. Should a random bullet take your life, the extra training or preparedness before deploying seems a waste. The inner conflict of this is seldom discussed but often processed in the minds of our soldiers: just another reason to appreciate the men and women who fight our wars.

In the case of our medics, they were sacrificing for the soldiers of the task force. Giving their free time to package individual medical kits was a decision to sacrifice their home family for their work family. The wives often have to process this fact. A wife kisses her husband on the cheek as he heads off to spend another Saturday of overtime readying for war. She understands the need to be exact and perfectly ready. She knows the extra preparation could make the difference and bring him home to safety. When he is ready, he then continues to work to prepare his buddies. Many of the wives see the decision as a choice between families. Most accept and understand and let him go. Other fears suppress the anguish of this choice. Nevertheless, it is there, and it is made, and it is just another reason to appreciate the spouses of the men and women who fight our wars.

Prior to deploying, the army completes a medical screening of all its soldiers. So in addition to getting the three hundred-plus man task force trained and medically equipped, we had to make sure they were healthy and that all shots were up to date. Having only experienced the regular army up to this point in my career, I gave little regard to the immunization issue. Until, of course, it came time for me to get my shots. The army Special Operations community was required to vaccinate against many more microscopic organisms, including rabies. Because of the awareness of the weaponization of small pox, every soldier was vaccinated or revaccinated for small pox. This was not without risks.

Small pox vaccination results in a systemic, or full-body, response as well as creating a significant sore, or pox, at the local site of injection. Small needles were used to infuse the vaccine into the skin. For those of us having been vaccinated as children, revaccination required 10–13 pricks with the vaccine-laden needle in order to ensure an immune response. The risk of infection at the site of the pox was the most likely of the adverse effects of vaccination. However, if soldiers touched the pox and then, say, perhaps touched their eye, small pox could be transmitted to the eye, resulting in the formation of a pox sore. The most worrisome systemic complication is viral meningitis. Doug, one of 160th SOAR's finest medics, had all the clinical signs of meningitis following his vaccination.

In the build up for Operation Iraqi Freedom, the 160th decided to grow its medical section by a few physician assistants. In its early years, Task Force 160 had utilized PAs extensively. But it had been a long time since the last PA served the regiment. Army PAs are extremely well trained and often function as independent providers, with minimal to no physician supervision. When I was attending the army flight surgeon's course, I met one of the best PAs with whom I have ever served. PA Rob was extremely bright and his medical knowledge was as good as any medical doctor. He was fresh from Afghanistan with the 101st Airborne Division, where he acquired medical planning skills that were second to none. The 160th itself evolved from the 101st Airborne Division and was thus collocated at Fort Campbell. Being stationed at the same post meant his move to our unit saved the army the tens of thousands of dollars it costs to reassign a soldier from another post. More importantly than his convenient location and medical prowess, PA Rob was a soldier's leader with an outstanding commitment to mission and men. Soon after meeting him, I resolved to influence the regiment to recruit PAs with him in mind as my future colleague in the 1st Battalion, 160th SOAR.

In only a few months after arriving at the 160th, I and the other medical leaders convinced the battalion and regimental commanders to hire PAs. We were also able to convince the Department of the Army's Human Resources Command's Physician Assistant assignments people to part with a few. So in early 2003, while both 160th SOAR and the 101st Airborne Division were tuning up for OIF, we conducted the first 160th assessment board for physician assistants held in a long time. While working through the army's process to change assignments, I kept Rob informed of our progress. When it came time, he, along with a few other physician assistants, came to 160th for an assessment. The entire process of an assessment to the 160th SOAR is considered confidential. However, the final portion involves an interview board. Senior leaders from the regiment sit in an intimidating fashion as the job seeker presents himself for questioning.

PA Rob had just finished his board when the senior regimental officer convening the board received an urgent phone call. He quickly left the room. I was the medical subject matter person present for the boards to ask questions regarding medical competency. At this time, I was still new to the unit. As this senior officer left, several of the other board members who had been in the unit for some time gestured for me to follow him. They all indicated that whatever that call was, the implications were that I needed to get my newbie backside to headquarters and see what was up. The remainder of the boards were canceled, and I ran to battalion headquarters.

Mark, the operations officer, and several others of his staff were stuffed into his small office in the battalion headquarters as I came in, once again huffing and puffing. CNN was broadcasting that a Special Operations helicopter crashed near Bagram Afghanistan, killing all four crewmembers. The typically phlegmatic Mark was visibly angry that CNN would broadcast this prior to allowing us to do the family notifications. The leadership of the unit had gotten the call within minutes of the crash. Within thirty minutes of the crash, CNN was showing pictures of a special ops MH-60K Black Hawk and announcing there were no survivors.

Reporters on the battlefield are a bittersweet reality for soldiers and their families. The benefits are obvious, as the people at home see how heroic the soldiers of the nation are, they connect with them, and develop a heart for them. The patriotic reception soldiers receive these days has a lot to do with the awareness the populace has for how difficult life in combat can be. Whenever Americans see a crash on television, their hearts bleed for the families of the lost soldiers. However, just the opposite is true for the wife of an army aviator. And for the wives of Night Stalkers, those feelings are amplified 100 fold. The difference between the regular army aviator families and the special ops aviation families is in the size of the force. If a regular army helicopter goes down, family members have some solace that there are a lot of army helicopters flying in the combat zone. When a Special Operations helicopter goes down, it can mean only one thing. Either your husband or your best friend's husband is involved—and probably dead.

When a Special Operations helicopter goes down, the wives circle the wagons. They call one another, knowing who is and is not deployed. They all go home but stay close to the phones, hoping that the crews who were not involved call home to tell their wife, "Hey, don't worry, I'm OK." While the army wades through an arduous process of notifying various commands and confirming who is involved, the wives go through a process of elimination. They often discover who was involved, and who is soon to be notified that their loved one is not coming home.

The 160th SOAR takes great pains to prevent this amplification of the tragedy for many reasons. Having your children's father and your best friend simply deployed is nearly enough stress for even the strongest person. The kind of family stress initiated by CNN announcing that a Special Operations aircraft has crashed detracts from the unit's ability to do its mission. When aviators are deployed, they think of their families all the time. Missions come and go, and soldiers focus on the mission when they need to. But when a crash happens, the men know what their wives and children are thinking back home. And knowing the anguish your wife is suffering can detract from a soldier's focus. In a sense, detailed messages that can allow the family to narrow down to the specific unit can create an increased sense of fear, worry, and for the soldiers deployed, increased risk. Further, putting families through that ordeal is just plain wrong, if it does not have to happen. Had CNN just reported a crash, the anguish would be significantly less. Narrowing it down to a Special Operations helicopter means a handful of ladies are on max "flight or fight" response for several hours, maybe even days. In other words, they have flipped into a high stress state dominated by adrenaline.

As Mark informed us of the names of the guys in the crash, and that there were no survivors, one of the names stood out to me. Greg, one of the crewmembers and a door gunner, had recently returned to Afghanistan. But not until after I, as his flight surgeon, had given him the OK to fly again. The flight surgeon has the interesting task of clearing pilots for flight.

Actually, the medical officer just recommends to the commander, who has the authority to ground the pilot. Most commanders do not go against the recommendations of the medical officer. Ultimately, that places the decision back on the physician. As physicians, we make life and death decisions often. But those of a flight surgeon in a combat aviation unit are a little different. I can say who does and does not go to war, who does and does not get put into harm's way.

Greg had a medical problem that had brought him home early from a deployment. While he was back at Fort Campbell, I treated his medical problem and kept him grounded from flight during the healing process. Aviators hate being grounded by the flight surgeon, and Greg was no different. He wanted to fly, and he wanted to return to Afghanistan and to his crew, who were fighting the war. His medical problem resolved, and I signed the papers, or his "up slip." That document meant he was well enough to fly. Two weeks later he is dead because of a crash in Afghanistan. Granted, had I not cleared Greg to fly, someone else would have been in his place in that aircraft. But the thought that I made the decision to put him up placed me a little too close to the concept of fate. I was uncomfortable with this for some time. I still think about it, and when I do, I usually quickly get the subject out of my mind.

The commanders dealt with the news agencies. I believe a call was made from somewhere because CNN pulled the story for several hours. As the command level above us worked through the decision on when to notify the four families, we began assembling the teams who would conduct the notifications. The operation would be planned with precision. The army had learned from its mistakes in making death notification during the early stages of the Vietnam War. Many people will recall the movie *We Were Soldiers*, starring Mel Gibson as the heroic Lieutenant Colonel Hal Moore. It is a true story of an infantry battalion's fight against a North Vietnamese Army regiment: eight hundred U.S. soldiers versus several thousand NVA regulars. The movie replicates the tragedy where death letters were delivered by Yellow Taxi Cab drivers in Columbus, Georgia. This actually occurred. Our unit psychiatrist at the 160th was in sixth grade and his father was stationed at Fort Benning, Georgia, when this happened. He recounts that he and his friends would be playing football and see a yellow taxi drive into their neighborhood. The play on the field would stop, the ball landing wherever as the boys looked with dread to see where the cab would stop. Invariably, one boy would see the cab arrive at his house and he would run home screaming and weeping while the others stood solemnly by. The leadership of 160th Special Operations Aviation Regiment would never let that happen to their people.

All notifications would occur simultaneously. If they were not simultaneous, as soon as one person knew, the other wives would immediately know which crew was down and thus who else had been lost. In the first van would be the chaplain and a commander or other lieutenant colonel–level leader in the unit. In a second van—held back a few minutes—were three people selected by the wife being notified and the doctor, carrying an antianxiety medication. When a soldier signs in to 160th, the wife is asked who she wants to be her support group if the unthinkable ever occurs. When we finally got the word to roll the vans, eight were assembled and staffed with the requisite crews. It is the mission you never want to go on and one you never forget.

What happened in the homes I visited that night will remain the secrets of the people who were there. In vague generalities, it is important for the nation to understand as much as possible what that wife goes through. She has seen the news, and she knows the van may come to her house. She waits. Looking dreadfully out a window, she sees two white vans rolling up her street, she begins to beg God that they drive on by, then feels the guilt of wanting it to be someone else and not her. When the van stops at her drive, she collapses to the floor.

The scene in the movie *Saving Private Ryan* comes to mind. The commander and the chaplain make the first knocks. The rest is sobs and tears and heart-rending screams. Fear of how she will care for her children, what they will ever know of their father, and all the other challenges of widowhood wash over her in an instant. While her husband has made the ultimate sacrifice, she and their children now, and for the rest of their lives, face the anguish of that loss daily.

I will never forget that night for as long as I live. And while the movies like *Saving Private Ryan* and *We Were Soldiers* attempt to, none can truly replicate that scene. *We Were Soldiers Once and Young*, the book upon which the Gibson movie is based, should be required reading for all Americans because it comes the closest of any to accurately describing the violent emotions of a family member to the news of a beloved soldier's death.

While every Lady Night Stalker fears this horrific notice, they learn to function with that fear just outside of their cognitive thoughts. They have to do so. Many of these wives have been through twenty-plus deployments because the soldiers and aviators of 160th rotate in for shorter, more frequent deployments. While the aviators impressed me with their bravery, so did these women, who were on again, off again single parents. Those who fail to develop coping mechanisms either divorce or the soldier leaves the unit. Those soldiers and wives who stay are tough women equally committed to the defense of freedom. Lady Night Stalkers are just as tough as Night Stalkers.

Planning for OPPLAN 1003 continued at a breakneck pace, despite the tragic loss of our fellow Night Stalkers. By this point in the process, the equipment not on hand was ordered and arriving daily. Kevin and Corey worked the additional equipment into the kits. We all trained on practice patients in the helicopters, ensuring we all knew where the equipment was located in the birds and how we would access it in the dark while in flight. Most of the medics had been doing these drills with Corey for years; some had conducted them for real in Operation Enduring Freedom. And while I had just graduated from one of the best emergency medicine residencies in the country, I was the person most being trained on how to do medical care in a helo in combat. For me, the issue was transferring the medical knowledge from treating trauma in an emergency department to the back of the helicopter. Treating a pneumothorax, a condition where air gets trapped between the lung and the chest wall, crushing the lung tissue, is an excellent example. In an emergency room, you just stick a needle in the chest of the patient and listen for a rush of air, confirming the injury. Listening in the back of a helo takes on new meaning. To adapt, the medics loaded syringes with water and attached them to the end of the needle. Instead of listening for the air, you watched for bubbles in the fluid in the syringe. Other senses are also less reliable in the helo. In the ER, I can smell blood or feces and know a penetrating object has nicked the bowel. However, in the helo, very few smells can overpower the gunpowder and jet fuel that wards off the enemy and fires the engines just above your head. My contribution during this train-up was subtle and more along the lines of challenging the medics to think about the science behind trauma and encouraging them to think outside the algorithms.

Prior to the events of Roberts' Ridge, Corey had an experience that shaped many of his training methods. He had just arrived the airbase at Bagram, Afghanistan, when a Marine CH-53 crashed in the mountains a short flight away. Corey and his flight surgeon at the time, Dr. Kyle, were tasked to join the quick reaction force (QRF) assembling to look for survivors. When they arrived, the scene of carnage before them would have paralyzed most people. There were wounded and dead marines scattered everywhere. Though the SOAR medics were the "in-flight medical stabilizers," Corey and Kyle felt obliged to help. They grabbed their medical aid bags and piled off the choppers. At nine thousand feet on the cap of a snow-covered mountain, these two men provided medical attention and initial stabilization to tens of wounded. In a matter of minutes, bleeding was stopped, splints applied, IVs started, and wounded loaded onto stretchers. The shooters on the QRF provided the manpower for the litters as the men were loaded on the MH-47s of the QRF. Corey and Doc Kyle continued treating the men in flight, crawling over shooters and equipment to give aid to the men despite their having developed early symptoms of acute mountain sickness while on the mountain peak.

Because of this horrific experience, mass casualty drills were planned and conducted as one of our last training opportunities prior to deploying to Operation Iraqi Freedom. The drills involved two to three medics. As the senior medic and trainer, Corey used a great deal of thought in the methods he chose. He never designated a leader. He would assign the three medics to the scenario, have them "stumble" upon 10–12 wounded people, and then watch to see which natural leader rose to the top. I and the other physicians of the 160th SOAR provided expertise on their triage and medical decision-making. But Corey's purposes were far more forward looking. Corey was concerned about the here-and-now of the upcoming deployment. However, having built the medical section of 160th to a great outfit, this hard-charging NCO wanted to ensure its longevity; he was always looking for the next leader.

The drills contained several critically wounded patients and then a larger group who were less severe. The medic's first decision was to triage who needed immediate medical stabilization and evacuation. Those patients who are expected to die regardless of your best efforts are left alone, as are those whose wounds were not life-threatening. Once narrowed to the critical but salvageable list, the medic begins to rapidly assess and treat the trauma. The standard trauma algorithms have for years mandated that the medical provider first establish a workable airway. This is known as the A in the ABCs of trauma management. However, in combat, this algorithm can cost a soldier his life. A large vessel injury through penetrating trauma can result in a soldier bleeding out his entire blood volume faster than a breathing tube or other airway mechanism can be emplaced. In combat, the medic has to think outside the algorithm. Therefore, SOAR medics were trained to first assess for massive bleeding, get a temporizing bandage in place, and then move to the airway.

The airway is nothing more than the tube through which oxygen enters the body and travels through the body to get to the lungs. The need to clear it of debris, and ensure the flow of air to the lungs, is intuitive. Frequently, that means inserting a tube into the trachea or, in medical terms, intubating the patient. However, the tube is only part of the system. The entire lung wall mechanism has to function for breathing to occur. Penetrating injuries to the chest frequently result in a "sucking chest wound." As the chest expands, air enters through the traumatic opening and penetrates the space between the lung and the wall of the chest. In some cases, the tissue prevents the flow of air back out of the chest. This leads to an ever-increasing pocket of air between the inner lung cavity wall and the lung tissue. As this air expands with each breath, the lungs are crushed. Patients with untreated sucking chest wounds die very fast.

The medic moves along his algorithm, treating emergencies as he goes. He places IVs and begins to give the necessary fluids to correct for blood loss. As the process unfolds, and as someone calls for an evacuation helicopter, the treatment begins to transition from treating wounds and medical stabilization to packaging the patient for the medical evacuation. At this point, the medic has to know exactly which type of aircraft is inbound to get his patient, what its medical capabilities are, and where and how he is going to get the patient into the helicopter. Will a hoist operation be necessary, or can the helicopter land? Does the patient need to be driven or carried to an extraction landing zone? Meanwhile, someone must secure the area — pull guard, if you will, defending against any enemy who might stumble into the gaggle of medical personnel. No one does this better then the Special Operations flight medics of the 160th Special Operations Aviation Regiment.

The final piece of training was to add our chemical protective garments, know as mission oriented protective posture, or MOPP (pronounced "mop"). The various pieces of the outfit are added with increasing MOPP levels. At MOPP level four, every square inch of the soldier's skin is covered. Everyone has seen movies where some biologic or chemical agent threatens civilization. These alien looking creatures from the Centers for Disease Control or some other government agency descend on the small town in their chemical suits to isolate the organism and treat the wounded. The army's protective equipment is just as cumbersome and significantly more uncomfortable. The suit contains charcoal and weighs a ton. It is always worn over the battle fatigues and, even in cold weather, the slightest tasks produce untold amounts of perspiration. The mask is Darth Vader–like. And, when sweating, which occurs any time the mask is on, no antifogging compound known to man can prevent the buildup of precipitation on the inside of the glass. The gloves are simply evil. Putting IVs in patient's small veins while wearing gloves similar to those used for stripping furniture is damn near impossible. Numerous studies by the military have shown dexterity degradation and metabolic energy demand increases in the order of 50–75 percent inside MOPP-4.[13, 14]

But unless you are interested in becoming the next patient, mastering how to provide medical care while wearing this astronaut suit, on top of being in the back of a blacked-out helicopter, is essential. And train we did. I will never forget when Cory put me on the spot and had me place two IVs into a mock patient in the dark, using NVGs while I was dressed in

MOPP-4. The pressure of doing that as all the medics stood around watching was different than passing medical boards, but it was no less daunting. After it was over, I felt as elated as I had upon graduating medical school.

As the final moments prior to the deployment neared, our equipment was checked and rechecked. With the to do list nearly zeroed, the leaders wanted to give the men some time with their families. There were numerous flights scheduled to airlift the task force, its aircraft, and equipment to our intermediate staging base. Once our names were slotted on a particular aircraft, we had a very reliable estimate of our departure time. In the two to three days prior to deployment, each soldier spent a considerable amount of time at home, readying his personal affairs.

I remember clearly the night my wife and family drove me to the airfield for my departure. At this time, we had no idea how Saddam's military would fight. We fully expected chemical and possibly nuclear weapons. My wife and I suppressed all fear for the sake of the kids and drove to Fort Campbell's airfield for my departure. The memory of the recent family notifications was stuck in my mind. I wondered how Camie would respond and how the kids would regard me later in their lives should I die in the sands of Iraq. I can remember as we drove in silence, picturing Alexa, my daughter, telling her husband about her father and his death in the war. It probably seems odd or strange in some way, but the image was not uncomfortable at the time.

When we arrived, the flight commander told us the air force aircraft had been delayed and suggested we return in a few hours. Camie and I took the opportunity and drove over to Charlie's, a Fort Campbell steakhouse with a regional reputation for outstanding steaks. The family enjoyed one last meal together, making very little small talk. We all knew what was next, and talking about how the flower beds looked seemed just a bit trivial minutes before leaving your family to go off to combat for the first time. After a very good steak, we headed back to the unit.

Our medical section was extremely supportive of one another. Whenever someone deployed, other members would come and assist in loading baggage, driving the deploying soldier to the airfield, and then sitting with them and chatting until the deploying soldier's plane was closing its doors. We pulled into the medical assembly area and the men were already loading our gear. I hugged each of the children, giving them the typical "Obey your mother" and "Don't worry about daddy, I am in God's hands" speech. I kissed my wife of fifteen years and told her I loved her. I told her I hoped that regardless of what happened, she would never regret having married a soldier. She responded in the steady fashion that characterized her, with, "You are fighting for us. I believe in what you are doing." Those words meant a great deal. I turned and walked away.

My wife and children drove slowly away. She recalls trying with great difficulty, but success at this point, to hold back the tears. I can only imagine her thoughts, and to this day, I have not asked her for any details. She does recount that as she and the children drove away, they could still see me in the rearview mirror. At this point my son, who was only seven years old, said in a soft and genuine voice from the back seat, "I sure hope daddy doesn't die." All efforts to hold back the flow ended, and both she and our daughter burst into tears. They were just down the road from where she dropped me off, but she had to pull over. After several minutes of sobbing, she and the kids headed away. Later that night, as aircraft loading was nearly completed, I called her on a friend's cell phone. She told me what our son had said. We said very little else, but just knowing she was on the line was relaxing. We said our good-byes. I joined LTC Jeff in the forward section of the C-5 for the long flight to the Middle East.

Chapter Six

The Initial Attacks

The air force C-5 Galaxy is an enormous transport aircraft with a lower section capable of carrying 270,000 pounds of supplies and equipment. The nose of the aircraft opens, and with the tail ramp down, you could literally drive right through the aircraft. In the rear and above the cargo area is a personnel section that has an eighty-one-person seating capacity. The second floor forward section seats another eight to ten people and is connected to the pilot's cockpit. This allows those flying in that section to communicate via the satellite communications system available to the pilots. LTC Jeff moved up to that section because of the need to communicate to command during the flight. As the flight surgeon and principle staff officer for medical issues, I often traveled with the commander. It frequently meant I got great accommodations, and this being my first flight, I was glad to accept the offer to join him there.

It was my first of several of these flights to OIF and OEF, and I must admit that nervous energy kept me awake for most of it. I read *Gates of Fire*, by Stephen Pressfield, a book about the three hundred Spartans who held off the entire Persian Army at Thermopile. It's a great book to read as you head off to war. Whether it is the U.S. Army veteran of Bastogne or the armor-clad warrior of the Spartan nation fighting off thousands of Persians, soldiers of today draw strength from the warriors of the past. When I was an infantry company commander slogging through swamps on some dreadful training mission, I often recalled the soldiers in Burma in World War II or those in the rice paddies of Vietnam. When my feet were freezing in some high mountain pass during winter training, I recalled Washington's men at Valley Forge. None of these men had Gore-Tex boots or moisture-wicking cold-weather garments. They only had their will and a passion to see our nation and the world remain free. Our indoctrination into the brotherhood of arms is filled with history lessons that compel us to press on.

I stepped off the C-5 in a remote region of "a neighboring Arab country," which allowed U.S. Special Operations forces entry, but wanted no official acknowledgement of its assistance. The ground was a fine red powder that conjured up images of Mars. Walking through the powder made me think I was walking in baking flour. The air was as dry as any place I ever visited – and the list of fun "vacation trips" the army afforded me over the years included the Mojave Desert. At the terminal where we disembarked, a sprinkler system kept a small lawn and two palm trees watered. They were as out of place as a Mafia don at a redneck wedding. We would later witness the lawn being sprayed with the collected contents of our Porta Potties. Needless to say, no one was caught sunning on the lawn. The airfield the country loaned us was near the border of Iraq and very isolated. The runway was extremely long, and the surrounding space allowed for our very large task force. Fuel points, ammunition storage areas, and other logistical pieces were already coming together as I arrived. Only about half of our task force, at this point known as Task Force 20, had arrived in the ISB. Very few of our special ops helos were on the ground. Air force Specter Gunships, A-10 Warthog and F-15 fighter jets, British fighter jets, and numerous other coalition aircraft were parked about the airfield with mathematical precision. It was the beginning of an immense city dedicated to but one purpose: the removal of Saddam Hussein from power and the return of democracy to the people of Iraq.

As we disembarked the aircraft, we were marched through the terminal and processed into the cooperating neighbor country. The country's soldiers were there to greet us. As we filed through, they asked for our military identification cards. I noted they were recording our Social Security numbers and prayed those lists would somehow be lost. Identity theft is a terrible thing for anyone. But for a physician it can be devastating if someone recreates a medical license and practices under it. I shudder sometimes with the image of the grinning Arab soldiers holding a list of American soldiers' Social Security numbers.

Intermediate staging bases provide units with last-minute opportunities to acclimatize, prepare equipment, load ammunition, and practice. Intelligence on enemy positions and morale are finalized, as are plans developed and refined. Our task force feverishly continued planning and rehearsing the upcoming operations. Our primary missions were to search for Saddam Hussein and to find his smoking gun, the WMD. In the days to come, Saddam would primarily be referred to as the Ace of Spades, or "BL-1," for "Bad List One." We were also tasked with locating other regime leaders and Saddam facilitators. There were several other support missions designed to assist the Rangers and other special operators, but these were small missions, usually with the unit's close air support platforms.

Life on Mars—as the place was not affectionately called—while not Spartan was a huge step down from what the special operators typically experienced. The Night Stalker medical team lived in a single hangar-sized clamshell tent. The cots touched; there had to be two hundred–plus people in this tent. It served as a holding area for soldiers, sailors, and air force personnel assigned to the Special Operations task force as they processed into the ISB. We lived in this facility for probably a week and then moved into our own sleeping tent. Our sleeping tent was approximately forty feet wide and perhaps eighty feet long. We partitioned it so that one end would serve as the medical facility. Our litters, medications, and medical equipment were arranged in makeshift fashion, giving the entry point of the tent the look of a rural emergency room. Further back and through a curtain were our living quarters. There were cots for sleeping, and over time, we slowly acquired some of the creature comforts of home, the first being a heating and air conditioner unit. After that came a television with satellite hook-up. An Xbox and DVD player were a standard part of the packing list for all SOAR medical deployments. These guys had deployment comfort down to a science. After approximately three weeks, washing machines arrived, along with a mobile kitchen trailer, MKT. The MKT could make T-rations, probably so named because the food was precooked and served from tin trays, where it was merely heated. Despite the recent advances made to the meals-ready-to-eat, a foil packaged meal used for field operations, three weeks or more of the same thing had everyone ecstatic to get hot food, even if it was precooked and served from a tin tray.

While the location seemed quite remote, it apparently was not remote enough. Just prior to the start of the shooting war, CNN broadcast our exact location to the world. Shortly after that broadcast, U.S. counterintelligence agents identified two Iranian intelligence operatives in the town near our ISB. Thanks again CNN.

Defensive positions (tents do not fair well in a missile attack) were difficult to create in the ISB. Further, the SCUD missile, which had created enormous fear in Saudi Arabia and Israel during Desert Storm, was believed to be still a part of the Hussein arsenal. There were other missiles with lesser range supplied by countries not respecting the embargoes placed on Iraq following Desert Storm. These were all capable of striking us in our ISB. For protection, the unit brought a number of concrete water conduits large enough for soldiers to run into should the call of "Incoming!" go over the PA system. These conduits were covered with earth and served as our only defense against rockets. As the war progressed, a very ingenious device called the HESSCO was used extensively. This cloth-lined collapsible wire cage was an easy-to-assemble barrier, and once filled with earth, became a nearly impenetrable wall. Iraq and Afghanistan are now covered with these amazing examples of ingenuity. Every military compound is ringed by rows of the larger versions of the HESSCO. Oh, to have invented it.

In the ISB, we continued simultaneous mission planning and training. The pilots would make a flight around the area to ensure the aircraft were undamaged in the airlift from the States. Corey would arrange for the medics to be on board. We flew as often as we could, practicing placing IVs and running various trauma scenarios in the back of the helos. Initially, we did primarily daylight flights, then transitioned to night flights. Meanwhile, the mission list narrowed, and the more probable targets were identified. Each mission was prioritized and the units handed the timeline for mission execution. The first major mission, named Objective Beaver, would be a hit on a suspected chemical and biological weapons facility. This prompted renewed training on both treating chemical patients as well as providing medical care while suited up in chemical protective gear.

The actual shooting war began for Special Operations two or three nights prior to the actual shock and awe kickoff. Following the 24th Infantry Division's "end around" flanking maneuver of the ground forces during Desert Storm in 1991, Saddam Hussein positioned strategic observation posts all along the Iraq–Saudi Arabia border. In order for army ground forces to penetrate that barrier undetected, those observation towers had to be taken out. The mission fell to the 160th's Little Birds and gun-laden Black Hawks, know as direct action penetrators, or DAPS for short. There were no assault birds carrying ground forces on these attacks, just the armed helos that were tasked with shooting up the towers, causing the Iraqis to run. Rockets and missiles destroyed the associated buildings. These missions were the first shots fired in Operation Iraqi Freedom. Once again, the 160th Special Operations Aviation Regiment led the way.

On the day of the formal initiation of the war, which would soon be known as the shock and awe phase, I ran into the signal corps (communications) officer in the 160th SOAR tactical operations center. He had been given a computer generated diagram showing the flight paths of the almost four hundred Tomahawk cruise missiles planned to land at various locations in Iraq in only a matter of hours. Of course, the cruise missiles were just a small part of what Saddam could expect, but looking at the interlocking lines and flight paths would make even the most seasoned air traffic controller nauseated. We realized we were currently situated very near the flight paths of a large number of the missiles. Some simple calculations told us what time to expect them, and we made plans to link up at a large Sea Land cargo container. At just about sunset, my friend and I climbed to the top of the container, broke out a couple of cigars, and watched the show. We did see quite a few, but it turned out to be less entertaining that we hoped. Deconflicting the flight paths of the missiles meant most were at very different altitudes and spaced to prevent midair collisions. It was a great thought, though. The smokes were good anyway, and the camaraderie was always gratifying.

During one of our training missions, I had the opportunity to meet a very energetic young sergeant who was the door gunner of the aircraft we were using to do some in-flight medical training. Glen was a great guy and was extremely helpful in getting us on board and set up for the flight. After we conducted our training aboard his aircraft during one of its test flights and were closing up the aircraft, Glen brought his personal aid bag or medical bag over to show me. He was extremely proud of the additions he made to his kit. He was trained up on how to use the extra devices and wanted my suggestions. The medics later told me that SGT Glen had turned down promotion at least two times so he could continue to fly. Seems he loved flying in the aircraft and door-gunning more than the thought of flying a desk as an administrator. His sacrifice of the rank and pay associated with the promotion would be very small in comparison to the price he would eventually pay for that decision.

Objective Beaver, my first combat mission, was a hit on a suspected WMD target deep in Iraq. The ground forces attacking from Kuwait were still almost two weeks from the outskirts of Baghdad, and we were launching an attack two hundred–plus nautical miles forward of those forces, requiring aerial refueling. The suspected WMD facility was west and north of Baghdad and was considered a possible primary site for Saddam's biological warfare program. Navy SEALs would assault and clear the target while a specialized WMD inspection team would search the target for the smoking gun, the proof that Saddam had chemical and biological weapons. Army Rangers were to provide additional security around the target.

Kevin and I were in an MH-47 as the primary CASEVAC platform. Our aircraft was third in flight order. As the lead elements landed at the insertion LZ, one of the MH-47s and one of the Black Hawk helicopters took enemy fire. The Rangers and SEALs all made it into their various positions and conducted the assault. However, in the initial assault into the LZs, the right door gunner of one of the MH-47s was struck in the right temple by an AK-47 round. The bullet penetrated his skull and exited at the back of his head. Since he was on another helicopter, Kevin and I were essentially unable to help. A combat medic on the aircraft began immediate first aid using the door gunner's very own first aid bag. The pilots diverted to an Iraqi airfield previously seized by Rangers. There, the door gunner was transferred to a specialized forward surgical team that had prepositioned there to cover our mission. The door gunner and a Ranger who was struck in the chest while being inserted via one of our Black Hawks were provided outstanding medical attention. Once stabilized, they were flown directly to Kuwait City.

The MH-47 with the wounded door gunner was too damaged to continue, so our aircraft returned to the LZ and retrieved both aircraft's contingent of SEALs. During the return flight, we were told the injured door gunner was not expected to survive. We also discovered that the inspection team found fresh bleach on all the surfaces of the laboratory. All the storage areas were empty, and there were no chemical or biologic weapons discovered. Everything had been wiped down with bleach, essentially killing any traces of biological weapons. And while the smoking gun would continue to elude us, the presence of fresh bleach was enough for many of us.

In the flight back, the command passed the battle roster number of the door gunner who was shot in the head. The battle roster was meaningless to me at this point. It was a number to let the people back at the base know who was wounded without passing the name of the aviator over the communications net. As we landed, I was still unaware of just who from our unit had been hit. I walked with Kevin over to the aircraft that was shot up and saw the first aid kit and listened to the combat medic describe what he did to stabilize the wound. Looking at the first aid kit spread all over the back of the aircraft, I immediately recognized it. Little did he know that just a day prior, as he showed off the additions to his medical bag, that medical bag would be used by someone else to save his life. SGT Glenn's flight to Kuwait was quick; he was immediately whisked into surgery. His long road to recovery was just beginning. However, the robust medical package provided by the Special Operations community was validated that day.

My first combat mission was a wake-up call in some ways. To this point, my youthful exuberance was unabated by fear.

But seeing my medic help the crewmembers of the shot-up MH-47 wash the blood of their friend from the helicopter was a terrible image that is still with me. As a physician, there are pictures in my mind I cannot seem to lose. Years of pronouncing people dead and then breaking the news to a family makes the process become routine. We all have a scripted statement to give. "Ma'am, we tried everything we could, drugs, CPR, shocking him ... and we just couldn't get him back. I am so very sorry for your loss." But there are images that just never go away. My first autopsy as a medical student was of a nine-month-old boy who died of sudden infant death syndrome. I can still see in my mind's eye the needle inserted into his blue eyes to remove the fluid in his eyeball for analysis. Perhaps the fact that my son was eleven months old at the time helped imprint the image on my brain.

Two images from that first combat mission plague me. I have made friends with their continued presence, just as I had to the image of the little boy. The first is the image of SGT Glen's blood being washed out of the helicopter. The other was of the men of his company standing at the back of the aircraft, weeping and praying for his survival. While I still desired the opportunity to prove myself in battle, to find some defining moment for myself, the costs of my desire became crystal clear that night on the back ramp of that helicopter. I begged God that night and many nights to come that no other soldier would be wounded in this fight. For me, the quest for the defining moment began to produce an inner conflict between the desire to prove myself and the appreciation of what that proof might cost.

As the war progressed, we watched the news coverage eagerly. The footage of the conventional ground forces moving up from Kuwait was informative. Some in the Special Operations community regard the conventional army with some criticism. Clearly, their training and their missions were different. The footage of firefights some of the units endured gave us all a deep degree of respect for the bravery and heroism of these young soldiers and marines. I say young, because in the special ops community most of the warriors have been around for some time, and some for a very long time.

News reports reflected the battles of conventional forces attacking toward Baghdad and the subsequent capture of Americans, including Jessica Lynch. The special operators took notice, but gave it little additional thought. We were busy conducting close air support to the special operators on the ground, as well as planning and flying missions similar to Objective Beaver. However, when the opportunity to grab a POW came along, everyone wanted to be a part of the mission. The SEAL team's commander got the mission early one morning as he and I were in the joint operations center making small talk over the coffee pot. The commander was shorter than most SEALs, but the diameter of his chest made up for his lack of height. He looked at me and said, "This will be the first chance to rescue an American POW since World War II." Without a word more, he hustled off to his planning tent to prepare for the mission. When the aircraft package was put together, it was extremely small. Further, the flight times from the start of the mission to the target were very short. A very short flight meant there was little a medical doctor could add to what a medic could accomplish. And as discussed earlier, additional supporters, even if they are medical, take away from the total number of shooters in the aircraft. Added to this was the fact that as soon as the SEALs finished that mission, they would return and launch on a hit to get Saddam, a mission requiring almost all the assets of 160th SOAR. Taken together, all these considerations meant the chances of me flying this historic mission waned to zero. I assisted minimally in preparing the medical package, but with the major portion of our unit staying in the ISB to prep for the follow-on mission, my staying put was the right thing regardless of the difficulty.

I patted Mike, one of our great medics, on the back and watched him depart. Another unique opportunity passed me by.

Mike was a quiet but extremely effective medic and noncommissioned officer (NCO). He was married and had a daughter he loved very much. He was extremely patient with both the women in his life, and I never once heard of or witnessed any disagreements between them. But once on the compound, or "down range," in either training or combat, Mike was as intense as any of our medics. As a medic, his skills were excellent, and his strength was pharmacology. When he and I would do sick-call duties in the medical clinic on the compound Mike would "pimp" me with facts on the drugs. In the medical field, we use the term pimping to mean quizzing someone's knowledge, and Mike would constantly challenge me with details on various drugs. He knew the aircraft and the unit extremely well. Mike's phlegmatic personality produced a Roy Roger–like attitude of "I never met a man I didn't like." Mike was as reliable as they come, and sending him on this mission was both a reward for his great service to the unit as well as a confidence that he could handle it, alone and miles from our medical team leadership.

The husband of a nurse working at the hospital where Private First Class Lynch was being held, known strictly as Mohammed, discovered Lynch while visiting his wife. He then traveled by some accounts as many as five days to reach a U.S. Marine unit, which passed the information up the chain of command. Mohammed then visited PFC Lynch two additional times, even providing sketches of her room's location in the facility. On the night of April 1, 2003, the SEAL team, with a contingent of Rangers from the 75th Ranger Regiment, assaulted the hospital. MH-6 Little Birds flew the assaulters to the target, while MH-60 Black Hawk's inserted the Ranger security force. The time on target was expected to be forty-five minutes. Lynch was on the helo headed home in twenty-five minutes from the time the Little Birds touched down on the building. This event was the first rescue of an American soldier from behind enemy lines since World War II.

The SEAL team, freshly returned from rescuing Jessica Lynch, immediately continued planning the ground phase of the assault for objective, or in military vernacular, OBJ PUMA. This was the second major combat operation on which I flew. The target was a Saddam palace located in the middle of Lake Thar Thar. Part of our task force, the gun-laden helos and the Air Force A-10 Warthogs assigned to assist us, would provide close air support with rockets and guns along the mile-and-a-half causeway out to the island. We were to fly approximately 250 nautical miles into Iraq and 200 nautical miles behind enemy lines, then land the team on the target. While the SEALs searched for Saddam, we were to move off to an isolated site in the desert and do race tracks in the sky. The last portion of this flight created a small amount of consternation because it was over water. Night Stalkers are outstanding flying over water, but it adds a few items to the checklist, for example a HEEDS bottle. This handy device — the helicopter emergency egress device system — is an oxygen tank the size of a small thermos. It is fashioned with a mouthpiece and regulator, much like those used by a scuba diver. In fact, just such a mission over the Atlantic Ocean produced more fear in me than any of my flights in combat. On my first overwater training mission, the weather was extremely bad, with high winds and twenty-foot seas. We were flying just above the water with night vision goggles on, and the pilot on the controls spoke over the intercom and asked how I was enjoying the ride. I told him my hand was on my HEEDS bottle, and he began to curse me out over the intercom, suggesting I had jinxed the flight. I was just trying to use humor to settle if not anyone else's at least my own fear. For him, it was not a joke. While most Night Stalkers are not that superstitious, the thought of crashing into dark water is petrifying, and at least this Night Stalker never spoke of it.

I clearly remember approaching Objective PUMA; we came at the palace from southeast to northwest. The degree of tracer and anti-aircraft fire was as fierce as I would ever see. LTC Jeff, in the jump seat just in front of me, commented that it looked like we were flying into World War II Germany. Add to this the spectacular site of the 160th's DAPs and the scene amped even the most stoic of personalities. On the way out of the target, after dropping the SEALs, a small boat located on the water and along our flight path opened up on us with a crew-served weapon, a large caliber machine gun requiring more than one person to operate. The bullets raked the left side of our MH-47 Chinook and pierced the Kevlar armor of the fuel tanks. Fortunately for me, sitting on ammunition cans just on the other side of that fuel tank, the bullet failed to penetrate the inner Kevlar wall of the fuel tank. Dave, the lead pilot on the aircraft, did a sort of waddle that evaded most of the gunfire and then lined up his left side mini-gunner, who quickly placed a few thousand rounds on the boat. The enemy gun was silenced.

The SEALs completed their tasks on the target, unfortunately not finding Hussein. We returned, picked them up, and started our long flight back to the ISB. The mission was conducted so far behind enemy lines we needed to aerially refuel on the return flight. While hooked to the Air Force C-130 refueling aircraft, an anti-aircraft missile was launched from the desert floor at the formation. Corey was on one of the aircraft hooked to the refueler. The MH-47 Chinook broke free of the fuel line and headed to just feet off the desert floor and the C-130 pointed to the stars. According to Corey, the missile came uncomfortably close to the Chinook.

The following morning, we were told we should pay close attention to the Central Command (CENTCOM) daily briefing from forward headquarters in Qatar. Central Command is one of the U.S. Defense Department's war management commands, with the responsibility for the Middle East and North Eastern Africa. H. Norman Schwarzkopf commanded CENTCOM during Desert

Storm; now, General Tommy Franks led the organization. We all gathered around the television set in our tents and watched as the entire mission for OBJ PUMA was described on CNN. Military graphics were shown to describe the mission, along with infrared video and night vision video; all showed the helos approaching and touching down on the target. It was easy to pick out our aircraft in the formation. The SEALs, who videotaped nearly all their missions, had supplied footage of their movement through and subsequent clearing of the target. The point was to counter the assertions from Hussein's television station that we were unable to penetrate into the country. The fact was clear: we could move anywhere in Iraq, and conduct any mission.

In early April, the command felt that seizing the Haditha Dam was a critical mission. The concern was that if Iraqi forces were to destroy the dam, the subsequent flooding and loss of water supply would lead to a significant number of casualties among the Iraqi people. The U.S. Army Rangers were assigned the mission and met stiff resistance in the attack. Following their seizure of the dam, the Iraqi military continued harassing them with small counterattacks and mortar fire for weeks. In the initial battle, one of the Rangers and perhaps a special operator assisting them were injured. The details of this engagement and the causes of the casualties are unknown to me; however, what I do know are the actions of the 160th SOAR aviators and the medic who responded to the call.

Doug was a single firefighter paramedic whose brother had enlisted in the army and found his way to 160th SOAR. Doug enlisted prior to 9/11, but when 9/11 occurred, the alignment of the stars and his fate led him to the 160th SOAR as well. Doug was the typical single soldier and spent considerable amounts of time chasing the things single soldiers chase. He had quite a reputation as a facilitator of social events, which he often threw at his bachelor pad. He purchased a home, something soldiers were doing more and more to grab some equity in real estate, and with it found a second calling. I am sure the stories I heard were embellished upon, but even so, Doug lived life large, and we were all happy for him. It's my understanding that Doug recently made a life change, became a committed Christian, and no longer hosts the social events described above.

Professionally, Doug tackled the role of Special Operations flight medic with the same degree of zeal he did his personal life. At the beginning of OIF, Corey sent him forward into Iraq with the Army Ranger unit assigned to our Special Operations task force. There, Doug served as a trauma medic at one of the early forward areas deep in Iraqi territory. When the call came from the Rangers for a casualty evacuation at the Haditha Dam, Doug was close by. He and a crew from the 160th launched, accompanied by a Special Operations surgical team. The aircraft came under significant fire as it approached the LZ, but the Night Stalker pilot was aware that the patients were in critical condition and pushed his Chinook into the LZ. As the patients were loaded, Doug rapidly assessed them and began appropriate medical treatment of their wounds. The surgical team assisted where they could, and as the flight continued back to the evacuation hospital, Doug stepped back and the surgical team moved over the patients, assessing his work and continuing the medical care. In a briefing in the Joint Special Operations Command Area the following day, the commander of the unit quoted the surgical team, who said of Doug, "These Night Stalker medics are the best Special Operations medics I have ever seen." Doug's actions on the rescue at Haditha Dam brought a great deal of honor to him and added to the already growing list of proud accomplishments of the Night Stalker medical team.

There was considerable debate on how the army would seize Saddam International Airport. The Special Operations community had planned since well before the war for the entire Ranger regiment, three thousand–plus soldiers to seize the airfield with a massive airborne and helicopter-borne insertion. By the time the mission needed to be conducted, regular army units were knocking on the door to Baghdad. The massive airborne operation was scrubbed, and a purely helo-based mission was planned. The regular army's 101st Airborne Division cleared the airport terminal as Special Operations troops, Army Rangers, and Navy SEALs cleared out the military hangar for Saddam's air force, their supporting buildings, and the elite Iraqi Republican Guards barracks located on the northwest edge of the military runway. As the assault began, elements of the Third Infantry Division cleared the streets just to the west of the airport.

The plan for 160th SOAR was to ferry the SEAL team and the Rangers into the airfield. As soon as the elements of the task force cleared their particular buildings, the focus shifted to establishing a forward base from which Special Operations hits could be done, looking for key regime members as well as the continued search for WMD. The 160th aircraft were to make several turns, or multiple trips. Initially, there was a plan for some elements to remain in Baghdad at the airport in the event the Navy SEALs had a quick mission. We needed a medical presence to accompany the initial ground forces into BIAP. Kevin and I served as the initial medical personnel for both the ground forces as well as the SOAR elements who were to stay. Thus, we needed a considerable amount of gear. The trauma mission was obvious. But moving our base of operation there would require both occupational medicine and routine sick-call medicine as well.

We prepared our equipment and loaded it onto a Skedco litter. The Skedco litter is a piece of plastic you roll up like a sleeping mat. When opened it can serve as a sled, carrying anything from ammunition to a wounded soldier. Since Kevin and I would need to support both the day-to-day medical care of the air crews who were moving to Baghdad, and provide medical care on missions flown from that new base, we had a significant amount of gear. All this on top of what he and I needed of our personal gear to survive in the area. It was planned that he and I should be able to live for a week without resupply. Because the WMD question remained, the command seriously considered that, as United States forces converged on Baghdad, Saddam might sadistically release either nerve or mustard gas on the assaulting forces as some martyrdom action. Consequently, as we assaulted the airfield, all shooters and ground personnel wore our complete MOPP-4 chemical protective garments.

The flight up was spectacular for me. Up to this time, my flights over Iraq were from the western regions of the country. On the flight into Baghdad, we turned southeast, and then back north, following the great rivers up and into the city. The illumination from the moon and stars was particularly good that night. For the first time, I could see in the shades of green in my NVGs what looked like lush vegetation, lots of palm trees, and obvious farm land. It was a significant change from the western regions. The tracer fires were more random than on Objective Beaver, Puma, and the others I had flown. These were only rarely aimed at the aircraft, and none hit us going into Baghdad. There were several very large explosions throughout Baghdad as we approached Saddam International Airport, soon to be my home for the remainder of my time in Iraq. These were obviously Air Force JDAMs, large two thousand–pound smart bombs that are guided by GPS, or Global Positioning System. Smaller explosions thought to be enemy mortar and 120 mm rocket fire were landing between the runways as we came in. The mission commander gave the "one minute call," and Kevin and I picked up our rucksacks, each grabbed a rope connected to our sled litter, and prepared for touchdown.

Saddam International is an enormous airfield. The main terminal splits the airfield into a military side to the west and the civilian side to the east. As the MH-47 Chinook helicopters landed between the taxiway and the main runway on the military side, mortar rounds from an Iraqi unit somewhere around the airfield landed just to our west. Kevin and I focused on getting into the hangar where the SEAL team and the Rangers would set up their headquarters. The sprint from the back of the Chinook to the hangar was a little short of half a mile. Kevin and I must have looked comical. Each of us was carrying on our back two rucksacks, one full of personal gear and a second for our personal aid or medical bag. We were in full MOPP-4, dragging a litter that weighed about three hundred pounds. The view through the three-inch-diameter circle of the chemical mask eye lenses quickly grew to half an inch as mine fogged from the perspiration. However, the mortar rounds still falling just a few hundred feet to our west gave us focus, and neither of us stopped for a breath until we were inside the Ranger perimeter and inside the hangar.

As we entered the hangar, it was clear the chemical gear was affecting everyone. One of the SEALs yelled at his buddy as we passed by something like "screw this shit," and ripped off his mask. Very shortly after getting into the hangar, the command gave the "all clear" sign, meaning the chemical threat had been downgraded and we were safe to remove our protective garments. Who knew or even cared if it was really downgraded. We just wanted out of those damn suits, and all I could remember thinking was, "Hell, I've got plenty of antidote, screw this mask and charcoal oven."

Kevin and I parked ourselves in the middle of a twin 747 hangar. It was dark, and there were very few others around. A small contingent of the Rangers provided security, while the SEALs moved to the far end of the building to set up a planning cell. Kevin and I let everyone know where we were in case anyone needed medical attention. Then we waited. To that point, I had essentially ran off the helo and sat down in the middle of huge blacked-out building. It was eerie sitting there with no awareness of anything around me. Something ten feet away could easily have been one thousand feet away. My life was for several hours was about three feet around me. The next day I would write the following in my journal:

Dropped into B-dad last night, darker than two foot up a bull's bum inside this hangar, sitting waiting for others to need my services and hoping for their sake they don't. Being dropped into a war zone in the middle of the night our world went from miles to a few measly feet. As daylight expands it grows, but in that initial darkness, all we know is our gear, and a few dark images around us. Kevin and I rucksack flopped and he handed me a granola and said, "Doc, we're Ranger buddies now."

A rucksack flop is where the individual just sits on the ground, never removing his rucksack and uses it as a backrest. The thought struck me, "Hey, Kevin and I are the first Task Force 160 medical people in Baghdad. Cool." What Kevin and I did not know was that the 160th element scheduled to stay, and for whom we were primarily there to cover the medical needs of, got held up. This essentially made Kevin and I the first guys from 160th SOAR to take up residence in Baghdad.

After a few hours of sitting and waiting, unable to sleep for the constant air force bombing throughout the city, I got up and started searching the inside of the hangar. Kevin and I needed a vehicle in order to transport casualties in case any of the Rangers got hit. He manned the gear and I cruised through the hangar, stumbling into a few sleeping Navy SEALs. As I moved around the outside of the hangar, I saw a very nice brand-new Nissan truck, which I felt was missing only one thing: "Night Stalker Ambulance" written all over it. Of course, we would never actually carve that onto the truck. But the image meant ownership and the benefits of having our own wheels. As I began to hot-wire the truck, a bearded fellow, dressed in a neat denim shirt and khaki slacks, came up and grabbed my shoulder. Considering the circumstances, I do not feel too wimpy to admit being a little startled by this. I imagine getting caught stealing a car in Nashville would produce an adrenaline spike, but in Baghdad on the night it fell to coalition forces, it damn near gave me a heart attack. The guy asked me what the blah blah blah I was doing. His English was outstanding, producing some degree of assurance that I was going to keep my head. I told him I was stealing this truck to be my ambulance. He informed me of the agency in the U.S. government to which he belonged and for whom he had already stolen the vehicle, and I felt immediately obliged to repair the steering column from my attempted hot-wire. I apologized profusely, which I think must have hit a nerve because the guy told me of a Nissan Maxima just down the runway that was also brand new and had the keys in the ignition.

Sure enough, only a few hundred feet down was a brand new, baby blue Nissan Maxima. The shipping plastic was still on the seats, and as he promised, the keys were in the ignition. Unfortunately, the car would not start. A quick look under the hood resulted in heartbreak. Someone had stolen the battery from the vehicle. I headed back over to the hangar and could see that the agency fellow was nowhere to be seen, but his nice truck was still right where he and I made our introductions.

The thought struck me that perhaps the Nissan truck battery would power the Nissan Maxima. Most physicians do research of some kind at some point in time. Whether in medical school as a project or as an endeavor to get into medical school, the scientific process is a right of passage. I happened to like doing experiments, and the research juices in my brain fired up as I contemplated the possible study I could make out of batteries in combat. My hypothesis was that a battery from one vehicle of the same manufacturer could be used in a different vehicle from the same manufacturer. Unfortunately, I had only one set of vehicles so my sample size for the experiment would have to be one. There were very clear risks and benefits to this experiment. There was a clear possibility that I would be the first to use the ambulance as a patient should I get caught stealing this guy's battery. The benefits were—besides having a new Nissan Maxima in which to sleep out the remainder of the night—that the unit would have a vehicle to transport wounded. Ultimately, curiosity got the better of me, and I made off with the truck battery without incident. Better yet, my hypothesis proved true, and the Maxima started immediately. I eased it into gear and drove into the hangar.

Kevin was clearly surprised to see the doc returning with a car. The fact that it had air conditioning, nice comfortable seats, twelve miles on the odometer, and a radio were icing on the cake. We notified the SEAL team commander we had an ambulance and told him where we wanted to park it. He appreciated the ingenuity and allowed us a place just outside the hangar to call home for the night. Through the rest of that first night, Kevin and I rested fairly comfortably in our new ride, listening to Iraqi radio stations interrupted by J-DAMs. We slept as much as we could, knowing that when dawn arrived, the units we supported would be hard and fast at their next set of missions.

Interestingly, about a month and a half after that first night in Baghdad, I drove over to the terminal to purchase a few personal items from the post exchange, or PX, which had set up shop on the civilian side of the airfield. The post exchange in the States is a department store on military posts where soldiers and their families can purchase items at a discount and tax-free. The company granted the contract to manage these is required to deploy to combat and field similar stores where soldiers can purchase personal items like snacks, sodas, and hygiene products. Essentially, they bring creature comforts to the battlefield for a price. In all my trips to OIF and OEF, I loved going to the PX for no other reason than watching people. The U.S. military is a multicultural animal, with people whose lives and work are as varied as any in our nation. You may see a typist from a finance unit standing next to an elite spec ops warrior, both in line to buy a case of sodas. On this day, I was at the PX looking for smokes. My cigar supply was running low, and I heard they were selling high quality cigars—meaning the kind that cannot be imported into the United States. As I was standing in line, in walked the bearded agency guy who had unknowingly loaned me his truck battery on the night I arrived Baghdad. Tragically, he recognized me and came over to chat. He asked me about the battery, and I confessed in a measured laugh, hoping I would survive the day. He blew it off, saying, "No worries, man, I had taken that battery from the Maxima I sent you to go drive, knowing it had no battery. You owed me." And with that, he walked off.

Important note: All equipment taken in the initial response and attack was reimbursed to the Iraqi people and government beyond its value.

Pictures

Portraits of Hussein were everywhere

Black Hawks over Baghdad

A Night Stalker medic and I next to an MH-60 K Special Operations Black Hawk helicopter shortly before capturing Saddam Hussein.

An AH-6 Special Operations Little Bird flying over "suicide alley."

**An MH-47 Special Operations Chinook launching flares
to avoid a missile shot.**

The author about to depart on a mission;
note the medical equipment in background.

An IED made from an artillery shell and pieces of metal, disguised to look like a road traffic barrier.

The Boeing 747 with no seats, allegedly used by Hussein to fly WMD to
Syria. Of note, the soldier posing in the door for this picture was the son of
an African American embassy worker released by the Iranian hostage
takers in 1979.

Visiting Baghdad International — no longer Saddam International.

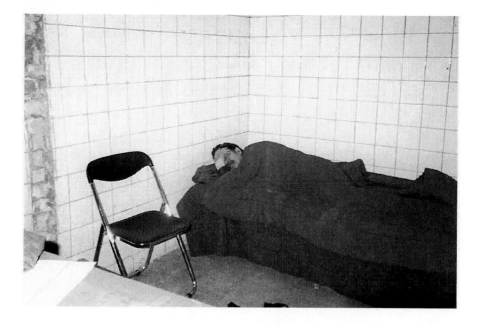

Saddam in his bunk on the night of his capture.

Picture of *Stars and Stripes* with my notes from the interview with Saddam on the night of his capture

**In Afghanistan, just prior to the mission
during which Pat Tillman was killed**

Chapter Seven

Finding the Bad Guys

The Joint Special Operations Task Force leaders had decided Task Force 20 would occupy the military side of the airfield. All the shooters and aviators centered themselves on a hangar large enough to fit two 747s, the same hangar Kevin and I occupied on the night of our arrival. The airfield and its terminal, now called Baghdad International Airport as opposed to Saddam International, became the home to our higher headquarters. Both the Joint Operations Center and SEAL Team Tactical Operations Center were located in the terminal area. The 160th SOAR, with its helos parked just outside the hangar, took up residence in office buildings attached to the side of the hangar. The hangar floor and adjacent rooms were covered in pigeon feces, in some places as deep as two to three inches. Many of the men voiced concerns over the health hazards. To comfort the men, I actually videotaped the mess in the event soldiers became ill from it and needed to prove these living conditions to the powers at the Veteran's Administration. Once it was cleaned, the place was not half bad.

Kevin and I occupied a room adjacent to the area where our pilots and crews planned their missions. This was an ideal situation because we could interact with the pilots, and we were always available to answer questions, provide medical care, or just BS with the guys. It was also great because when a mission happened we were right there and in on the planning from the very beginning. The 3rd Infantry Division and 101st Airborne Division had essentially secured Baghdad by this time, and Kevin and I felt very safe cruising around the airfield. We found a few palaces and outfitted our medical station with a few pieces of furniture from one of Saddam's plush residences. These served as a waiting room of sorts for those visiting the doctor. On one such outing in our Nissan Maxima, we came across an infantry battalion from the 3rd Infantry Division. I recognized a major who, as it turned out, had served with me in 82nd Airborne Division when I was an infantry officer. Ed was a very thin infantryman who looked more like a computer technician than an infantry leader. However, I remembered him as a real warrior from our 82nd days, and we hit up a great conversation about those good ol' days. I told Ed we needed a truck or something like it to better serve as an ambulance. While the Maxima was comfortable, it was difficult to place a litter or stretcher in the back seat. Ed was aware of a brand new Nissan truck that his guys could not get to run. Kevin and I followed him to his designated base area and discovered that the battery was missing. The truck looked very familiar to me, but as it turned out it was not the agency guy's truck. Kevin and I then set out, found a battery across the airfield from another friend, and returned to Ed's. Once a decent battery was in, the thing fired right up. That pick-up became the "hooptie" that drove the task force medics all over Baghdad. It didn't take long for Kevin and me to equip ourselves with the items necessary to care for the wounded in our aid station and during transport in our new vehicle. Our acquisitions were timely, and the missions began again in earnest.

In January 1991, on the first night of the air war portion of Desert Storm, LCDR Michael Scott Speicher was shot down over west-central Iraq in his F/A-18 Hornet. His body was never recovered, and at the conclusion of the conflict, he was listed as "Killed in Action—Body Not Found." However, a thorough investigation followed, leading many people to believe Scott Speicher was alive and being held in Iraq. In late 1991, after the war's conclusion, Iraq returned remains they said belonged to a pilot named Michael. DNA analysis confirmed they were not Scott Speicher's remains. In 1994, U.S. intelligence identified the crash site and asked the Iraqi government to allow an onsite inspection. In late 1995, the Iraqis allowed a flight investigation team to travel to the site. The team did not reveal the location of the crash site to the Iraqis until the night prior to their search. When they got to the wreckage, it had been "expertly searched within one month prior to the team's arrival." The wreckage revealed that Speicher had likely ejected and not crashed with the aircraft. Further implicating the Iraqis was a flight suit supposedly found by a Bedouin boy near the crash. Forensic analysis determined that the Iraqis had planted the suit. In the build-up for Operation Iraqi Freedom, intelligence agencies reported an American was being held in a Baghdad prison. President Bush even mentioned LCDR Speicher in a speech he gave the United Nations in the fall of 2002 while arguing for regime change in Iraq. Many people believed that American to be Scott Speicher.[1]

As soon as the Navy SEALS had established their headquarters areas, they immediately began planning a hit on the prison. Elements of the 3rd Infantry Division's Cavalry Squadron were asked to assist. For the young infantry and cavalry soldiers, the opportunity to work with Navy SEALs and the Joint Special Ops community was a real highlight to their OIF experience. The mission used tank and infantry armored vehicles to establish a breach into the walled compound. I remember very clearly the rehearsal for the mission. The 3rd ID Cavalry guys looked and acted like kids in a candy store. Very few soldiers get a glimpse into the black side of Special Operations. Most go a full twenty-year career and never even know the myriad organizations in the country's spec ops community. It was neat watching their excitement. The SEALs were also pumped for the mission. Having rescued Jessica

Lynch, the opportunity to find a navy man held hostage for so long meant a great deal to these dedicated warriors.

The mission was standard operating procedure for the SEAL team. The only difference this time was their transportation. Instead of flying in on 160th SOAR helos, they would blast into the compound in Abrams tanks and Bradley fighting vehicles. The SEALs would then conduct a standard take-down and search. Unfortunately, by the time the assault forces stormed into the prison compound, someone had opened the gates and released the prisoners. It was a discouraging mission for the SEALs. With no other intelligence on Speicher's whereabouts, the men moved on to the next mission, which would nearly cost the life of a dear friend and fellow physician.

By this time, another Special Operations medical unit had arrived in Baghdad, and a good friend of mine, Dr. Trey, was sent as the medical officer on the mission. He traveled along with several other supporters in an M-113 armored personnel carrier. The thing is essentially a metal box on tracks. As the unit moved down an elevated street, the M-113 slid off the side of the elevated road, flipping onto its top and coming to rest in a water-filled irrigation ditch. The vehicle quickly filled with water. The men in the back were unable to exit through the blocked top hatch. In the dark water, unable to find the handle for the door at the rear, the men were trapped with no ventilation. Trey later recounted that he and the men trapped inside had only five or six inches of air between the top of the water and the upside down floor of the vehicle. They were discovered roughly thirty minutes after the accident. As the men were rescued, Trey went unconscious from oxygen deprivation and carbon dioxide excess. CPR was conducted on him, and he was quickly revived. Trey would later recount that only he "could find a way to drown in a desert." The loss of this great friend, physician, and warrior would have devastated the unit. Trey and the Special Operations community "dodged a bullet," or in this case a lot of water, that night. Thinking about

Trey's possible loss made us all realize just how dangerous these missions could be.

Abu Abbas, an alias for Muhammad Zaidan, was the founder of a paramilitary terrorist group known as Palestine Liberation Front, or PLF. Throughout the 1980s, Abbas's organization conducted attacks on both military and civilian targets throughout Israel and Lebanon.[2] However, he is most infamous for his 1985 hijacking of the Italian cruise ship *Achille Lauro*. During the hijacking, wheelchair bound American Jewish passenger Leon Klinghoffer was rolled to the edge of the ship, shot in the head at close range, and his body and wheelchair thrown overboard. After the hijacking generated enormous worldwide outcry against the PLF and its parent organization, the Palestinian Liberation Organization (PLO), Yasir Arafat directed Abbas to change course. Abbas, using coded radio signals, directed the terrorists to pilot the boat to Egyptian waters.[3]

Yasir Arafat went into the diplomatic role and negotiated with the Italian government and Egyptian government, essentially stalling an opportunity for a rescue. Subsequently, the ship was able to reach Egyptian waters, where the Egyptian government allowed the hostage-takers to depart the ship unmolested. The terrorists were allowed to fly from Egypt to Tunisia.

During the hijacking of the *Achille Lauro*, Joint Special Operations Command was mobilized, and none other than the same SEAL team currently working in Iraq was called on to do a ship take-down and rescue the hostages. However, the boat arrived in Egypt prior to the team getting approval to do the take-down. Much to their chagrin, the men of this elite SEAL team began to redeploy. However, President Ronald Reagan authorized an aerial intercept of the Egyptian 737 flying the terrorist to Tunisia. Six F-14 Tomcats, the navy's premiere carrier-based fighter, intercepted the 737 and forced it to land at

Sigonella, Sicily. There, after being turned around in flight, Navy SEALs converged to take the terrorists of Abbas's organization into custody.[4] One of the Navy SEALs who took part in that mission was my chief resident during my emergency medicine residency. He had gotten out of the navy, gone to medical school, and did a residency in the army. Talk about a small world.

When the 737 landed, the SEALs went into action, cordoning off the plane, surrounding it with a double ring of armed warriors, and positioning a headquarters element beneath the plane. However, within an hour of doing so, nearly three hundred Italian police and military units surrounded the SEAL perimeter. The Italian leaders, which included a three-star general, demanded they be allowed to conduct the arrest as the cruise ship was Italian and they were currently standing on Italian soil. Over the next twenty-four hours, the hostages and two additional dignitaries sat on the 737 with a ring of Navy SEALs facing in and a ring facing out, toward the Italians. Three hundred–plus armed Italians surrounded the SEALs. As negotiations on how to handle the situation progressed, it became clear that Abu Abbas, the mastermind of the hijacking and a senior leader of the PLO and head of the PLF, was one of the "diplomats" on board with the terrorists.

In what would be his political undoing, the prime minister of Italy, Bettino Craxi, caved to Arafat and allowed the 737 to fly to Rome, where Abbas was to be given an Italian air force officer's flight suit. Abbas was escorted to a Yugoslavian plane that set up to transport him from Rome.[5] Ultimately, he evaded justice and returned to live in Tunisia. The SEAL team went home empty-handed. In the next election cycle in Italy, the Craxi government was unseated and his replacement immediately orchestrated a trial resulting in five terms of life imprisonment for Abbas, the mastermind of the hijacking. In Tunisia, where Abbas was living at the time, the ruling government expelled him, and he fled to Baghdad. There,

Saddam Hussein sheltered him from Italian and U.S. authorities.

Having been unsuccessful in finding Scott Speicher, the SEAL team turned its attention to finding Abu Abbas. Unable to take him into custody in 1985, the men were resolved to bring Abbas to justice. In the days that followed the prison raid, as the Special Operations presence at our new base at Baghdad International grew, the team executed mission after mission on intelligence that continued to lead nowhere. Then on April 14, acting on what was believed to be good intel, the SEAL team, along with elements of the 160th, did a hit on a small house in Baghdad. I was in the JOC in the airport terminal speaking with medical leaders about the medical plan for a mission set for execution the following day and watched the assault via the camera in a Predator drone flying over the target. The hit was a daylight mission with a time-on-target of 1300 hours (1 PM civilian time). The hit was again unsuccessful or, in military speak, a "dry hole." However, the people on the target were interrogated, and within a few hours, another hit was scheduled. At 1700 hours, a second assault was made, and a few friends and I were again in the back of the JOC watching the assault unfold on a big screen TV. This time, however, Abu Abbas was found. He had $45,000 in a suitcase, along with several different passports. He later admitted he was just about to depart the house for Syria. The SEAL team had finally settled an eighteen-year-old score with Abu Abbas.

On a subsequent mission involving an element of the SEAL team currently serving in Iraq, one of the SEALs became a casualty. We did not participate in the mission on this rare occasion. It seems that upon entry into the target, the lead SEAL fired his shotgun down a dark hallway. The pellets hit the side of the wall, causing several of them to ricochet back and into the SEAL's face. The velocity of the shot was significantly reduced and all the pellets remained embedded in his lower face and jaw. We knew nothing of the mission or the injury until the

SEAL walked into my medical office area in the hangar. He said, "Hey doc, can you dig these out?" I grabbed a Petzl headlamp, an eighteen-gauge needle, and slowly began removing the shotgun pellets from the SEAL's face. On numerous occasions, I asked if he wanted me to numb the skin with lidocaine, but he refused. I dug probably fifteen pellets out of his skin, most of which were so deep you could not see them, only feel them. The guy barely winced, never shed a tear, and never took a single pain pill. Special operators—they are just that damn hard.

Having conducted the majority of the hits early on in OIF, it was time for this SEAL team to turn its responsibilities over to the army's elite counterterrorism unit. The unit had been conducting operations in western Iraq, along with conventional forces. It was now their turn to serve as the main assault element of TF 20. Kevin and I continued touring the area. One of many odd findings in those days was the aircraft of Iraq International Airlines. There were three planes in total, one Boeing 747 and two Boeing 727s. One of the Boeing 727s had not fared well in the initial assault on Saddam International Airport and was mostly a burned-out hull situated on the military side of the airport. The two remaining aircraft were parked on the northeastern end of the terminal. We were able to access these two and discovered that the planes had their seats removed and cargo flooring installed in them. They essentially were converted to cargo aircraft, despite the obvious markings of the passenger carrier with Iraqi Airlines. At the time, we thought nothing of it.

In 2006, years after I returned from Iraq and the same year I resigned from the U.S. Army, a book by Georges Sada, air vice marshal in Saddam's military, was published. In it, Sada, who was an advisor to Hussein and very high in the Iraqi government and military, states on multiple occasions the Iraqi military, on orders from Hussein himself, used WMD on his own Iraqi people. Sada asserts that Hussein would conceal the use of WMD by giving the order "special mission with special weapons."[6] General Sada states that in every case where those words were used, chemical and biological weapons of mass destruction were employed. Perhaps the most interesting part of the book to me was Sada's account of how Hussein got the WMD out of the country.

On June 4, 2002, a three-mile long irrigation damn near Zeyzoun, Syria, collapsed, killing scores of people living in three villages downstream. As aid workers from all over the region converged in Syria, Hussein saw an opportunity to rid himself of the evidence.

> Posing as shipments of supplies and equipment sent from Iraq to aid the relief effort, were Iraq's WMD. Weapons and equipment were transferred both by land and by air. The only aircraft available at the time were one Boeing 747 jumbo jet and a group of Boeing 727s. But this turned out to be the perfect solution to Saddam's problem. Who would suspect commercial airliners of carrying deadly toxins and contraband technology out of the country? So the planes were quickly reconfigured.
>
> All the passenger seats, galleys and toilets, storage compartments, and other related equipment that would be needed for civilian passengers were removed, and new flooring was installed, thus transforming the planes into cargo planes. The airliners were then used for transporting hundreds of tons of chemicals, armaments, and other paraphernalia into Syria under the cover of a mission of mercy to help a stricken nation.[7]

The planes were there at the airport in 2003 when we took it, devoid of any seats or passenger areas.

With the arrival of the army's counterterrorism unit, the pace of missions picked up, with the fresh faces and attitudes of the newly arriving operators. TF-20's primary mission at this point was locating the high-value targets, or HVTs. The targets were a group of people most wanted by the American and Iraqi governments. As mentioned before, the top fifty-two of these were placed on the face of a deck of cards, called the Iraqi House of Cards. The higher the value of the target to the United States, the higher value the card on which he or she was placed. Saddam, being the ultimate catch, was placed on the ace of spades. The operators and planners simply began referring to the targets by the card and not by their names.

On April 29, almost three weeks after our occupation of Baghdad International Airport, the physician assigned to the army's counterterrorism unit came to see me about a mission they were planning. His unit had some evolving intel on the king of clubs, Izzat Ibrahim Al-Duri, and a hit was being prepared to take him. Al-Duri was an Iraqi military commander and the vice president of Saddam's revolutionary council. His loyalty to Hussein and the Ba'ath party was unquestionable. He was one of three original plotters who brought Hussein to power in 1968. He was implicated as the main architect of the chemical shelling of Kurdish villages in 1988, resulting in the deaths of more than five thousand civilians.[8]

The counterterrorism unit's physician, also named Kevin, noted that Al-Duri had a significant medical history: hypertension, or high blood pressure, heart disease, diabetes, and leukemia. As he was a family physician by training, Kevin sought me, an emergency physician, out and requested that I accompany him on the mission. At this time, the army's counterterrorism unit had insisted that their doctor go in the aircraft on the missions. I, of course, was grateful for the opportunity. However, while I had treated numerous heart attacks and diabetic crises in my emergency medicine residency and had the knowledge base, in Iraq I lacked the medications to treat these effectively. In our medical planning, the one thing we overlooked was the HVTs. I never anticipated caring for diabetics with known heart disease because the troops I typically cared for were all in phenomenally good health. On my subsequent deployment to Iraq, I was better prepared for this contingency, particularly when the Ace of Spades mission occurred. But my medic, Kevin from the 160th who was flying the mission with me, began a search for the medications that would allow us to handle a nontrauma medical crisis like a heart attack.

Our friends from the air force provided a solution. Just down the runway, the air force was establishing its initial base occupation plan and had constructed a small hospital. I was able to borrow a cardiac monitor from them, which could do an EKG, or electrocardiogram. Our monitors only tracked key vital signs. This device could help in the event of an acute heart attack. They also had nitroglycerine that we could employ if Al-Duri got chest pain from coronary artery disease, a precursor to a heart attack. I scrounged a few other medications, and we had the makings of decent plan of attack should he require attention.

The operators got a possible location for Al-Duri on the thirtieth, and the mission launched just after dark. The two Kevins and I were in the JOC when the mission started. The CASEVAC aircraft for the mission was just outside the JOC, ready to go if word came that either the shooters or the HVT needed a doc. As the lead elements of the counterterrorism unit breached the target, a member of the HVT's entourage randomly sprayed an AK-47 down a hallway. The bodyguard was immediately engaged and killed by shooters storming the complex. However, this burst of gunfire tore into four of the operators. The call for the CASEVAC followed immediately. With four patients, we added an additional Black Hawk and launched for the target. Kevin from the counterterrorism unit was in the lead aircraft, while Kevin from the 160th and I were in the back aircraft.

Three of the wounded were less serious. Two of the three were shot in the chest, but the body armor deflected the bullets.

They essentially had very large and painful bruises to their chest walls. The fourth soldier had a bullet wound to the upper part of his shoulder, where the ricochet from his chest plate struck. However, one of the soldiers had a belly wound, and Kevin, the counterterrorism unit doctor, directed him to our aircraft. From a medical standpoint, this operator had a rare injury. As the operator was loaded onto the aircraft, we got a little basic history from him. He had an AK-47 round enter his abdomen just below his navel. There was no exit wound. He kept repeating over and over again, "I can't feel my balls, doc." He had lost sensation in his genital areas and down his entire right leg. Further, and although to the operator it was less important than the loss of sensation to his genitalia, he could not move his left leg. Loss of feeling on one side, with loss of strength on the other, means only one thing: a spinal cord injury known as a Brown-Sequard Syndrome. Dr. Charles Edouard Brown-Sequard discovered the syndrome in 1840 after experiments in which he cut half of a spinal cord.[9] The injury is extremely rare and most often results from a stab wound. We flew the patient immediately to a forward surgical team that had set up shop in the terminal at BIAP. There he went immediately to surgery. As it turned out, the bullet had impacted very close to the cord, but had not severed it. The pressure from the bullet interrupted the functioning of his spinal cord, generating the clinical picture of this classic injury pattern. The last I heard from reports from Germany, where the soldier was eventually evacuated, he was walking and sensation was returning. Based on his voiced concerns when we first picked him off the target, I am confident the soldier was pleased with that piece of his recovery.

As medical personnel in combat, we did not want patients. We preferred to be bored. Any other scenario meant our people were harmed. However, when the soldiers were injured, it created moments that defined us. How we acted and how we responded was not unlike how a soldier reacted when confronted with an ambush. We conducted medical drills very similar to what our brother shooters did for each type situation. And when it was all over, and when we had done a job we were pleased with, we patted ourselves on the back and whooped and hollered, much like I had seen the shooters do after they took down a target or an HVT.

It seems unsettling even to me to think of celebration in a situation like that, but in a sense, that is what medicine is. As physicians, whether in combat or not, we live in the midst of disease, pain, and emotional heartache. We gather strength from the challenge or the uniqueness of a particular case. We even remark, "No one wants to be the exciting case on grand rounds." It usually means you have a unique or rare disease. This operator was my first casualty in combat. As a Special Operations physician, we rarely had patients to care for; our people were just that damn good. But when we did, we relished the opportunity to make a difference, and we felt good, not about the soldier's injury, but about the opportunity to have our split-second decisions matter.

My first look at Mosul came on an early morning mission to find Huda Salih Mahdi Ammash, the five of hearts on the deck of infamous Iraqi most wanted. As Saddam's principle scientist for biological weapons, Mrs. Ammash was a high value target.[10] The Army's 101st Airborne Division would assist us in conducting the mission. It would not be the last time the Screaming Eagles would partner with TF-20. Later, they would assist TF-20 in the assault on Uday and Qusay Hussein. I flew up to the division planning area for the 101st in the early night of May 3. We met leaders of the division, who directed us to an infantry battalion further down the Mosul airfield. There we linked up with mission planners and worked out the details of the assault. Coordination within a single unit for a combat assault is tricky. Doing so between two units that are so different in their operational techniques is absolutely critical and painstaking. It was dark when I arrived in Mosul, so my appreciation for the differences of the northwestern part of Iraq would have to wait.

Derik, a new medic in the 160th, had shown himself capable of an invite to the big dance. Normally, medics had to serve in the medical clinic at the 160th compound for a few years deploying to training exercises and slowly proving themselves to Kevin and Corey the senior medics. Derik joined Kevin and me within a few days of our getting to Baghdad. His nickname was Big Mac; he was a large fellow with an equally large personality. He and Doug were good friends, and Big Mac would frequently be a part of the social gatherings at Doug's place. His operational security skills (his ability to keep a secret) in regard to these parties were a bit lacking, and the stories about these parties most often came from Derik. He looked very young to me, but he was extremely bright, and I recall him quoting the formula to calculate intracranial pressure in a head injury during a lecture someone gave on the subject as more senior medics looked on in admiration. He was equally fearless in battle, always working the leadership to get himself on the most difficult missions.

Special operators from the army's counterterrorism unit planned the "action on the objective" and then gave the Screaming Eagle infantry battalion commander the locations for his blocking positions. We launched, carrying the operators, while the 101st Airborne Division's helicopters flew the infantrymen to their blocking positions. The target turned out to be an extremely large complex of buildings within a few miles of the northern Syrian border, and clearing each building took an enormous amount of time. During this time, the lift helicopters were forced to do racetracks in the sky several miles from the target. As daylight peaked over the horizon, we could see lush green grass and fields with rolling hills and streams in nearly every valley. On the horizon, probably into Syria in one direction and Turkey in another, purple mountains were a sight for sore eyes for a crew living in brown, dusty Baghdad. The beauty of the place reminded me of the green in Ireland and back home. It seemed like an entirely different country. We landed once to refuel our smaller Little Birds, and the grass looked like wheat and was nearly waist high. I commented in my journal about the smell of the grass. It was a treat to see this contrast from the dry, dusty south.

Our mission did not turn up the scientist. However, the result of the mission was informative. On numerous missions to grab key people from the Hussein regime, the act of searching was often enough. As it turned out, Mrs. Ammash just escaped prior to our arrival. Later, after considering a life on the run from Task Force 20, she decided to turn herself into authorities.[10] She was remanded to U.S. interrogation forces. I am unaware of what happened to her after that. But it is important to know that some missions would seem like failures, only to have them prompt either the HVT or others to cooperate.

As we continued mission after mission, with most aimed at the lesser faces on the most wanted deck of cards, the missions grew more and more routine. Life in the hangar had not improved much. Many of our troops still slept in an area filled with pigeon excrement. Hot food and a porcelain toilet could have significantly lifted morale. My days had turned into routine sick-call, a bit of a deflation for this former airborne infantry commander turned emergency medicine doctor. I never wanted any of our people hurt, but I was as much an adrenaline junkie as any of the shooters and pilots. My adrenaline came from saving people's lives. My inability to do that—even as I was comforted that none of our people were harmed—led to a sense that we were not needed. We often spoke of the enemy getting hit so we could save them, achieving the rush. This thought, while gruesome, allowed us to believe our skills would be employed, while not on any of our own.

Toward the end of May and near my time of departure, LTC Jeff decided to reward the men of the task force with a little something extra. Our resupply bird was coming from the States, and he made a call to the rear and had the logisticians pack all the fixin's for a good ol' fashioned barbeque. It is not hard to understand missing something. I think it is hard to understand sometimes how even the simplest gestures matter so much to people. We were deprived of a lot of things when deployed: our families, our everyday routine, and the finer things of life in the United States. Leaders who go the extra mile in a situation like that make a reputation for themselves that outlasts their tenure. Even to this day, the men of the 160th SOAR speak of LTC Jeff's BBQ in Baghdad as if it were a million-dollar prize personally delivered by Miss Universe. He is fondly remembered as one of the best leaders the 1st Battalion ever had. That BBQ summed up LTC Jeff's philosophy: Take care of your people, and your people will take care of you.

Soon after the BBQ, the unit began rotations back to the States. In the 160th SOAR, there is always someone deployed fighting the War on Terror. No other unit in the military can do what the 160th does. Therefore, they have remained deployed 365 days a year since the very beginning of OEF and OIF. They cope by rotating pilots and crews in and out for shorter durations. A crew may deploy for sixty days and then return for 120 days back in the States, only to rotate back for another sixty days of combat. The unit can manipulate the timing for a soldier's deployment because the 160th SOAR has its own dedicated air force transport to each theater every month. If one soldier has a son graduating high school, he may wait until the following month to go. In the end, the members of the 160th spend more time deployed than anyone. However, they manage it so that people can have as normal a life as possible, when it really is impossible.

On June 4, PA Rob landed in Baghdad. I took a day or so to orient him to the area and introduce him to the British SAS and army counterterrorism guys we were working with at the time. It was most important that the customers we flew to and from their objectives understood there was no compromise in the care their men would receive. I knew there would not be. But they needed to know that. On late June 6, I packed my gear into two large duffle bags and an army "large ALICE rucksack." My medical bag was replenished with meds I thought the guys flying back may need. We gathered in the twilight of the sixth and sat on our gear, awaiting the command to load and depart.

As I sat on my duffle bag waiting to load it was hard to contain the excitement. All of us had huge grins on our faces. We were headed home. The fight to that point had not been that bad. The 160th SOAR had only taken one combat casualty, SGT Glenn from our very first assault mission into Iraq. The two main counterterrorism units we served in the opening days of the war took only one serious casualty, the soldier I picked up from the Al-Duri mission. And the Rangers who supported these two elite Special Operations units only had a handful of casualties themselves. We had separated our aviation assets and functioned from up to five different locations simultaneously. Medical personnel had flown with the operators on every mission and supported them in an unparalleled fashion. Further, not a single soldier was sidelined for a DNBI illness. As the sun faded in the distant sky, I thought of the men who were wounded and thanked God for their survival and his mercy on the unit. The memory of the missions and our success warmed me. The opportunity to be a part of this historic action gave me a sense of pride. The coming anticipation of seeing my wife and children shifted my thoughts from Iraq to home. Soon I boarded an Air Force C-130 and flew to Kuwait City to start the first leg of my long trip home.

Chapter Eight

Home and Back Again

Returning to the States was quite an adventure. We took a military aircraft down to Kuwait City and from there boarded a charter civilian aircraft for home. In Kuwait, we got the opportunity to visit the Kuwait International Airport. This was a fascinating view into Arab culture for me. The food court was not unlike any you would see in an American mall. Kuwaiti businessmen passed in European suits as well as traditional Arab garb. In our military fatigues, we seemed to attract a broad range of looks, from obvious disdain to large smiles and thumbs up. Once through the requisite inspections, we were ready for the commercial flight home.

Our contracted aircraft was a small commercial airliner from a similarly small airline. Consequently, instead of the routine single layover in Spain or Germany, when we flew air force aircraft, this plane stopped in Crete, Ireland, and Newfoundland. Imagine eighty warriors who have been in relatively austere conditions stepping off an aircraft at a civilian terminal. If you guessed the beer tent was the first stop for everyone, you are spot on. Ireland was especially nice. Having bought the entire aircraft its first round once airborne, I was told my money was no good. That meant for me, when my Guinness was emptied, another very quickly took its place. While the exuberance of coming home was intoxicating enough, the beer heightened our level of enthusiasm. Once in Canada, we decided not to drink alcohol anymore. We assumed the command would have the families present for our return. Stumbling off the aircraft with your kids ready to welcome dad home would have been in poor taste.

Seeing your family for the first time after the fear of never seeing them again is quite indescribable. My son and daughter bum-rushed me, mauling me with hugs and kisses. Camie was more reserved but glad nonetheless to see me. On the drive home, the kids filled me in on all their adventures while I was away, which included getting two new Labrador retrievers. As I would later discover, new dogs were a common acquisition for Lady Night Stalkers while husbands were deployed. My better half sat silently, driving. The thing I remember the most was the enormous color change. Iraq was shades of brown. Brown buildings, brown dusty deserts, and even the trees were brown with dust. As we drove home in June, the lush Tennessee forests streaked by at 75 mph. The new colors were tipping me into sensory overload. I literally closed my eyes for fear of having a seizure.

When I returned, all of life was like that: sensory overload. For the first weeks, catching up on all the missed information, stories, food, family purchases, and the "honey-do list" was a bit challenging. While you cannot wait to make up for lost time, the challenge of returning from combat is difficult. First and perhaps foremost, your friends are still in combat, laying their lives on the line, and you are at home sleeping in your own bed. There was always a twinge of guilt in a lost part of the mind. At times I was distracted, wondering what missions the guys were flying and if they had all the medical coverage they needed. That distractedness characterized the entire time I was back and complicated the home life.

Adjustments at home are nearly equally difficult. The parenting dynamic and leadership dynamic in the home is significantly altered when the father deploys to combat. I am sure the challenge is equally difficult when the soldier is a mom, but I can only relate our experience. In my absence, my wife became the sole decision-maker. If she wanted to purchase an item, she could not pick up the phone and call. If she wanted advice on a reward or punishment for the children, getting my opinion was not an option. On my first deployment, we did not have e-mail or phones so there was no contact. She, in essence, became a single parent. Over time, the children adjusted to this and even expected it. Then dad returns and expects to be a part of decision-making and have his authority as head of the home placed back on his shoulders the minute he returns. Fortunately for us, my wife's father, a two-tour Vietnam veteran, had warned us of the dynamic. Even still, it was difficult for all to settle back into a comfortable rhythm. I recall my son even answering me once when I directed him to do something with, "Well, I better check with mom first." Army Ranger dads are challenged by a response like that. We survived it, but not without adjustment.

My children drank up every minute of time I could give them. Subsequent deployments would be different. However, after the first, both my son and daughter relished their special time with dad. My daughter and I found that Starbucks was a mutually enjoyable experience. We would grab a book from the local bookstore, cruise over to Starbucks, and grab a caffeinated beverage. As typical of most teenage girls, hers was a sweet frothy chocolate concoction and mine was always the quad shot espresso typical of people who have marched through marshes as infantry officers or stayed up forever studying human anatomy. My daughter and I would just sit there, rarely talking, and just read. She is a consummate reader, and for her it was special to just sit there with dad and share what was special to her.

My son had decided while I was away that he wanted to play golf. Golf? I absolutely hated the sport. While some people lose balls, I, in my frustration, often lose clubs! Not really, but

I have bent a club before. I am often frustrated at work, so why be frustrated in my off time? But he wanted to play, so we went. He had not even held a club at this point. I at least had a lesson or two, so I tried to show him how to stand, grip, and swing. I am sure it was humorous just watching me attempt instruction, but when he took a swing before I could clear the area behind him, I know everyone on the driving range was rolling with laughter. As my son followed through after the swing, his driver came around and crashed full force into the bridge of my nose. I had just returned without a scratch from very intense combat operations with some of our nation's most elite Special Operations personnel. And within three days of returning, my son plants his driver squarely between my eyes, breaking my nose and what pride I had left. I sat down, half laughing and half crying. We joked about that for some time.

Despite some heart connections with the family, I still struggled to pull myself mentally away from the fight. Even on dates with my wife, my thoughts would wander to what the guys were doing. Always in my mind was, "Am I needed?" Occasionally in my mind was, "Am I missing something special?" Even having now gone to combat, I longed for that defining moment, but not selfishly. I would never compromise family, others, or myself for such a moment. But as I mentioned earlier, soldiers want to have an experience that quenches the thirst to know that in a crisis moment they would respond appropriately and bring honor to themselves and their country. I do not want to say it is a thirst for glory, but it is something akin to it. I reiterate: it is not a thirst for killing. Whatever it was, my first trip to Iraq failed to satiate me, and I sat at home distracted, not wanting to leave my family, but longing for something more.

Meanwhile, back in Iraq, PA Rob had such an experience. Rob had a lovely family. They were all staunch Christians who attended a vibrant church just down the road from us. His two girls were as energetic as he and as pretty as his bride. Rob seemed to always find a way to get jobs done but still spend a lot of time with the family. On Sundays, his crew would often head to Nashville for family night at the famous Wild Horse Saloon. The Wild Horse often hosts Country Music Television specials, and on Sunday nights, the establishment gives free line-dancing lessons to families. It is quite a riot, and his family often found its way there for some good ol' fashioned country music, dancing, and family fun. Rob had already been to combat with the 101st in Operation Enduring Freedom. He was a part of the conventional army forces that took part in Operation Anaconda. Now assigned to the 160th SOAR as the 1st Battalion physician assistant, Rob was making his debut in the Special Operations community. And his big day came in support of the assault that ended in the deaths of Uday and Qusay Hussein. Rob will, I am sure at some point, bounce grandchildren on his knee and tell them that story. I will leave it for him to tell. But it was a moment in history, and he was there.

Rob returned to the States shortly after the hit on Uday and Qusay, sometime around mid-August, 2003. Another Night Stalker physician assistant took his position, and he and I were finally located in the same place. Rob and I were the only medical officers assigned to the first battalion, the unit tasked with providing the leadership of the special ops aviation in Iraq at that time. The second and third battalions of 160th SOAR were busy supporting missions still ongoing in Operation Enduring Freedom. While another of the regiment's medical officer's assistance to our unit deployed in Iraq was appreciated, we both felt uneasy not being there with our guys. It had nothing to do with the medical competence of the guy covering for us. It was purely an ownership sense we had. We wanted to be with our team.

Sometime during this first rotation back home, the unit was placed on alert for a possible mission to grab two senior Al Qaeda leaders. They were discovered via classified means to be hiding in Mogadishu, Somalia. I was called to the operations officer's planning area in the 160th SOAR headquarters and briefed on the intelligence. After getting the initial intel dump, all the staff officers went about planning the packages, the staging areas, and the support needed to fly from Fort Campbell, Kentucky, and at precisely the right moment, conduct a Special Operations night assault to grab these two key terrorist leaders. For all of us, the mission to return to Mogadishu, the site of one of the bloodiest Special Operations battles in history and the place where the 160th SOAR lost two Black Hawks and almost two full crews in 1993, stirred a varying degree of emotion.

Having read the book *Black Hawk Down* several times and seen the movie, I was fairly well aware of the unit's history in Somalia. What I did not know or understand were the operational pieces that would be necessary for us to provide medical coverage on a return mission. Corey advised me that the unit kept all its lessons learned files in "the vault" at regimental headquarters. The file was easy enough to find — several people had reviewed it already in preparation for this mission. As I read over the files, the hair on my back and neck rose. Looking over the maps and their yellowing tactical overlays created a combination of excitement and foreboding. Here was the unit's history in my hands, and I was thrilled to see the real artifacts from the mission. I wondered who in the future would look at my staff planning for OIF and feel the same. As I began to appreciate the difficulties the unit faced conducting the Somalia mission in 1993, my concern grew, particularly since we would be going in very fast with as small of a "signature" as possible. That meant very little medical support.

As planning progressed, the intelligence on the exact location of the two Al Qaeda leaders began to grow cold. No hard location of the two in the city of Mogadishu ever materialized. The covert intelligence personnel working diligently to develop the situation there ran out of options and eventually the planning was canceled. The files from the previous mission were resealed and placed in the vault for some future flight surgeon and other SOAR staff should the opportunity resurface.

My wife and I were in the process of building a new house. We anticipated its completion in October, and clearly, my preference was to stay and help my wife with the closing. However, October was the time when either Rob or I needed to return to Iraq. Leaving my wife with the house was not appealing, but asking my PA to go back sooner (he had just returned in August, and I had been back since June) was even more difficult. But the wrench in the system was Christmas. Had Rob gone in October, he would be home for Christmas. If I went, he would be deployed over the holidays. I gave him the choice. And as fate would have it, the choice he made significantly changed my life. So, in October 2003, I launched for my second trip to Iraq.

Leaving for combat the second time was significantly less stressful than the first. I believe my wife was dreading the single-parent role more than the possibility of my death in combat. While that later thought never really left either of our minds, we thought less of the chance that I might die and more of the arduous task of her fending for herself and the children alone.

By now, the flights to and from the war were routine for most Night Stalkers, who had gone back and forth to Afghanistan for well over a year. Each month, the 160th was allowed one air force transport to ferry troops and equipment back and forth to the war zone. This allowed the unit to rotate soldiers in and out of the war zone frequently. As I described earlier, the conventional, or non-Special Operations army, does a twelve- to fifteen-month rotation into the combat zone. This usually allows them to stay home twelve to twenty-four months prior to redeploying. The routine for 160th SOAR was fairly simple. Command would be given the flight arrival time, and we presented ourselves with our gear. The families rarely even saw us off on the repeat shuttle runs to and from the war zone. It became routine for the soldier to drive himself, while another soldier brought his vehicle home to the family. Then, just before his return, the wife took the soldier's vehicle out to the compound and left it, not staying herself for any formal greeting. The flights were typically air force C-17s. The accommodations were not nearly as nice as Delta Airlines, but the flights were by far more comfortable. We always carried a sleeping mat on board, and shortly after takeoff we would roll out the mat between the various chained-down cargo pallets. We would snuggle up in an army poncho liner, a quilted camouflage woobie much like Linus's blanket of the Charlie Brown cartoon series. Ambien, a sleep aid, was issued to all soldiers for the flight over. Traditionally, we popped one and went to sleep on takeoff. We arrived at a layover in Spain or Germany just as the drug wore off. During the mandatory four hours of crew rest for the air force transport pilots, we hit the local brew pub, guzzled down a few German beers or Spanish wines, and then hopped back on the transport. Another Ambien, and seven to eight hours later, as the drug wore off, we touched down in OEF or OIF. Delta Airlines's customers never had it so good.

Chapter Nine

Al Qaeda — A Brief Distraction

Second deployments are somewhat easier than the first. Initially, you know the month you are scheduled to return. About thirty days from your intended rotation date, the U.S. Air Force supplies a three- to five-day window when it believes the aircraft will show up. This monthly aircraft is dedicated to the unit, and each month takes the next rotating group of operators, aviators, and support staff back to the sand box. Up until the actual date range is given, the deployment is less on the family's mind. But when the date is set, things begin to happen.

The soldier/father starts focusing on getting his gear together and assessing the ongoing missions in the combat zone through secure e-mails and other communications. Further, his mind begins to ready itself for combat. The fear factor escalates at home, and the whole family sits on pins and needles. Conflict can often follow. As the husband prepares himself mentally for the intensity of focus demanded in combat, his sensitivity meter often gets turned off. The wife, on the other hand, realizes she will soon be alone, responsible for parenting, household operations, and for many, her own employment. Her expectations tend to increase, hoping the husband will do more to make life easier for her, knowing she will soon have to do everything herself. Mix all the new expectations with the coming separation and feelings of fear for the husband's safety, and it can be a trying time. There comes a point for most families as the date draws nearer where everyone just wants it to happen. Then the soldier leaves, and all are wishing they had a few more days together.

Families ultimately develop their own systems. As deployments come and go, the coping mechanisms refine themselves. Those who never develop a coping system often divorce, separate, or leave the military. My wife and I were accustomed to separation when I was an infantry officer. But that had been years ago, and while medical school and residency meant many hours of disconnectedness, it only meant one night away from home for call duties every third or fourth night. We suffered through the same issues that all families do during the adjustment phase. Leaving the second time was fraught with fears and frustrations for both of us. Nevertheless, we managed.

By the time I returned, our task force had changed names from TF-20 to TF-121. I assumed the change was for operational security reasons, to keep the location and activity of our Special Operations task force as quiet as possible. Honestly, I never really gave it a second thought. The compound I left in late June was now a thriving city, with all the creature comforts of a well-established forward base of operations. The hangars previously used by the British SAS guys were now converted to well-equipped workout facilities. There were port-a-potties instead of the slit trenches dug by Ranger entrenching tools (a handheld shovel that has not changed much over the past fifty years). A new dining facility was churning out two hot meals a day, including a steak and lobster night each week. Compared to the men at Valley Forge, we were treated like royalty. The SOAR medics had moved into a combined medical treatment station with the joint headquarters medical forces. It made for easy living. They had a big screen TV, and we each had private sleeping areas. However, it meant we were no longer living and working alongside our aviators in the hangar.

The camaraderie between the aviators and the SOAR medics is absolutely unparalleled. The army medic has always been loved by his fellow soldiers. In fact, the first winners of the Medal of Honor and the Distinguished Service Medal, the nation's highest and second highest awards for valor in combat, were awarded to medical personnel. However, the SOAR aviators and their medics have a bond unlike any seen in the army. There are many reasons for this bond. Predominantly, I believe this connection comes from the fact that the medics of 160th believed themselves to be members of the crew.

It was a cultural mind-set cultivated by Corey, the senior medic. Even before Corey's actions on Roberts' Ridge, he set a command environment that impacted every person in the platoon of medics serving the 160th SOAR. If there was maintenance needed on an aircraft, the medics always pitched in. Even the docs got involved. I can remember many times carrying small fuel bags off the MH-47 Chinooks in order to refuel the Little Birds. This team mentality led to a reciprocal feeling from the crews. As word spread of the deeds of the medics in saving pilots' and crewmembers' lives, the bond was cemented.

TF-121 had two major missions when I returned. Most of the original deck of cards had been captured. Of course, the Ace of Spades remained at large. Securing him was clearly the number one mission. However, the insurgency was now clearly underway. Ba'athist insurgents, who had been joined by Al Qaeda operatives and their foreign jihadists, were now the second mission. TF-121's unique abilities for surgical strikes meant they would find themselves conducting many of these raids.

We conducted several hits to capture key people with intelligence on Hussein. Most were low-level players. There were several sheiks who agreed to help. Several of them were prepared to identify Hussein if they ever found him.

Unfortunately, none of these leads produced a score. However, the jihadists were increasing their organized activity, and by the middle of October were providing plenty of opportunities for special operators and aviators to excel.

On October 31, my good friend and fellow ER doc, Trey, who had nearly drowned on one of our earlier missions in Baghdad, started the day by visiting the airport terminal. Trey had the responsibility of caring for the task force's headquarters personnel and the detainees in the battlefield interrogation unit. This was my first visit to the main part of the civilian terminal since returning to Iraq, and this place had undergone quite a transformation, too. Trey and I sipped Turkish coffees in a shop at a café in the terminal, visited the post exchange and grabbed some Burger King at the soldier's shopping area. Trey was leaving the following day for Afghanistan and a renewed push there to find Osama Bin Laden. As soon as we returned, the unit was scrambled to the planning bays for some juicy intel. Apparently thirteen or fourteen visiting jihadists from Yemen had supposedly called home the day prior to tell their loved ones good-bye. Seems they had plans that would result in their acquisition of the promised seventy-two virgins. Their location was quickly identified through classified means, and 160th SOAR, the army's elite counterterrorism ground unit, and the British SAS were tasked to take these guys out. The mission was nearly a forty-five-minute flight from Baghdad. The army's counterterrorism ground unit medic, Mike, and I would provide medical coverage on an MH-60K Black Hawk situated on a friendly helo pad just a quick hop from the target. We had two armed Little Birds as escorts and as close air support to the shooters on the target.

The unit conducted several missions from the location, where we sat idly waiting for the shooters to do their thing. A unit from the 1st Infantry Division graciously gave us room on their landing pads. In previous missions, we had discovered the location of their chow line and where to get hot coffee. I took the medic, and we chatted with the folks in their tactical operations center while we gulped down some army coffee.

I developed a great deal of respect for the counterterrorism unit medic I was working with this night. Prior to 9/11, Mike was a firefighter, paramedic, and ski bum from Colorado. As the towers fell, he immediately signed up to serve his country. He had a connection with some people in the army's Special Operations antiterrorism unit and made the call. They assessed him and took him right on the spot.

Now, it's very possible the guy was feeding me a line of crap. However, he had the look of a ski bum, with artificially blond hair that was clearly not army regulation, and the skills of a seasoned paramedic. So if it was a cover, it fit well. You never really knew with these guys. They worked covers, and to keep it intact, they would keep it up even with other army people, even fellow special ops people. Mike was easy to get along with. Many of the people from Mike's unit were type A to the tenth power. Mike was extremely laid back, never judgmental and quite friendly. Later in the war, I heard he was awarded a very high medal for his efforts to save marines in Fallujah. I was never able to confirm the exact medal awarded. I did read the citation written by his command for the award, which detailed his heroic actions. The dude kicked ass regardless of the award.

As dark arrived, we headed back to the helo and prepared for the mission. All of the aircraft were cranked and blades were turning. Since most of these missions never required us to do more than just sit there, we often drank coffee and told jokes, commented about the families back home, or, as we say in the army, played grab-ass.

As we were grab-assing on the flight pad, I noticed a rocket streak into the sky, followed by some tracers. No sooner had I asked if anyone saw it than the British SAS, who had the mission to breach a portion of the enormous target, passed the code word that they had casualties. In seconds, we were airborne and headed to the target. From the calls made by the SAS medic on the ground, he had four casualties, and one was a head wound. As the men rushed through the door following a breach charge, the enemy detonated a delayed explosion. The first SAS soldier through the door took the brunt of the explosion in the face. The other three were filled with shrapnel, and one of those had a GSW, or gunshot wound, into what looked like his pelvis.

As the pilots began discussing with the ground personnel where we would land to get the casualties, Mike and I got our medical gear ready to treat the patients. This meant opening IV fluid bags, connecting the tubing, and setting up other equipment. We were advised that the landing zone, or LZ, would be hot, which for Night Stalker pilots and crew was no big deal, but for the flight surgeon it was. As I have recounted with many people since then, I'm fairly certain my sphincter tone could have crushed coal and made diamonds. As we came into the landing zone, the good guys were placing heavy suppressive fire on a building about one hundred feet from where we were touching down. A Bradley fighting vehicle commandeered by the operators fired a TOW missile at the building. The missile went high and streaked fairly close to our spinning blades. Mike immediately jumped out of the helo and began searching for targets on the building. Meanwhile, the good guy's suppressive fire was ricocheting all around us.

We sat in this awkward position for what seemed like five minutes, but was probably more like thirty seconds, and the patients never arrived. Then came a call from the SAS medic, who said he was not yet ready to load the patients. The entire crew chimed in, saying, "Great, so why the #$@& are we sitting here?" Our pilot quickly "un-assed the area" (an army term meaning get the heck out of Dodge) and we were airborne, headed to an aerial release point to do race tracks in the sky until the Brits had their guys ready to load. The medic on the ground was struggling to save the life of the SAS guy hit in the face. Getting four casualties packaged for transport is not easy in the middle of a firefight like this. We understood, but the aircraft and crew were put at risk before the men were ready. As we lifted off, a good buddy of mine, Dave, flying an AH-6 Little Bird, made a gun run on the building. No one was concerned about the proximity because we knew it was Dave. From a dive, Dave could hit a gnat flying 50 mph with his Little Bird's .50 caliber machine gun. Later the following day, Dave and I shared a cigar on the roof of the medical building. I asked him if he had let the young captain accompanying him in the aircraft fire as we were on and off the target. Dave's response was, "Doc, that wasn't a JV night." Later in the war, Dave would be awarded the nation's second highest medal, the Distinguished Service Medal, for an act of unbelievable bravery under intense enemy fire. That award is second only to the Congressional Medal of Honor.

After a few circles and what seemed like ten minutes, the Brits called us back to the target. As we touched down, we could make out two men carrying two wounded men in a fireman's carry and another hobbling toward us. They dropped the three patients and took off. We asked where the fourth patient was, and we were advised that the medic on the ground had opted to call off efforts to save the man who took the blast to the face. He had worked for a long time, trying to get an airway established in the dark, but could not. The SAS troop was driven to a medical facility and pronounced dead.

Meanwhile, Mike and I had three patients. Two were shrapnel wounds to the extremities. One was a GSW to the upper thigh, very near the pelvis. I took the GSW, and Mike took the two extremity shrapnel injuries. My initial concern on examining the patient was the lack of an exit wound. The bullet entered the inside of his upper thigh in his groin region. There was a high possibility that the bullet traversed the pelvis, severing arteries, which would bleed into the pelvic cavity. These injuries are deceptive because the pelvis can hold a lot of blood, and there would be minimal bleeding from the entry wound. The patient was talking and alert, so the A in the ABCs was clearly not an issue. I stuck a wad of Kerlex, a special type of bandage, into the entry wound and then placed an IV in his anticubital fossa, the area opposite the elbow. I ran a liter of normal saline wide open, pushed 10 mg of morphine, and then mixed an antibiotic. In the civilian world, antibiotics were not routinely given when a patient first presents with a GSW. However, in combat we often did so because of the nature of the environment. This brave Britton potentially had a very serious injury, and I knew he did not want an infection that close to his genitalia. Most soldiers can stand about any wound as long as that part remains fully functioning.

The patients were tucked away fairly quickly, and Mike and I gave each other a complimentary nod. The flight to the combat support hospital in Baghdad took about forty-five minutes. Our pilots called the hospital, advised them about our patients and their wounds, and got last-minute instructions on the landing site. Flaring into their helo pad was interesting; it was lined with four wheelers. Mike and I stepped off the birds and were greeted with three of these, each with a stretcher on the back. The SAS guys were each loaded onto a four-wheeler and hurried off to the combat support hospital's emergency room. This was none other than the famous Baghdad ER, where a friend of mine from residency would later star in the HBO special of the same name.

As we headed back to the target, the adrenaline rush of the mission began to ebb away. Mike and I sat motionless in the back of the Black Hawk as the pilots discussed where we were to park and wait for the next call. In the relative calm of the moment, my mind recalled a question I had asked my son several weeks before returning to Iraq. He and I had been camping, and I asked him what he thought the most important thing in life was. His response was to "grow up, get a great job, work hard, and make a lot of money." At the time, I knew

I needed to address the self-centeredness of his comment, but when you're about to depart for combat, you do not want your last words to your child to be a lecture. Pulling wounded men off a target on a hot LZ will make you regret not saying a lot of things. More importantly, I worried that my son's response was only a reflection of what he had seen me model. For most of my adult life, my passion had been to help advance what I believed was the service our nation provided mankind: freedom. No country on the face of the earth, in all of history, has advanced peace so diligently as the United States of America. America has freed a lot of nations from tyranny, and all we ever ask for is a place to bury our dead. My passion in my early years as an officer was to serve my nation and see the world free and prosperous. But after residency, I allowed a few moonlighting jobs and other activities to distract me. When I asked my son the question, I never intended for it to haunt me. But bullets whizzing by your head can bring different things to the forefront of your mind. As I sat in that helicopter, I realized I had in some sense gotten off track from my true passion. My yearning to see freedom advanced was not obvious to my son; I was not modeling it. As we neared our helo pad back at the 1st Infantry Division's compound, I thanked God for allowing us to survive the mission, thus giving me an opportunity to model something different for my son when I got the chance.

But unbeknownt to me, God was already working on my children. At the exact moment I was returning from the mission, my children were walking down a Clarksville, Tennessee, street in the usual Halloween ritual of trick or treat. The kids noticed a mother yelling at her child to stop running. The young girl was probably in fourth or fifth grade, but instead of stopping, she charged into the street and was struck by a car. The event got the attention of both my children. It was a brief moment for them to contemplate the gift of life and the responsibility to do something special with it. Life, or as I see it, God, has a way of getting our attention and redirecting us to what is important.

And while, for most of my life I had sought the elusive challenge of a defining moment in combat, this mission made me realize it was not about me. Life was far more valuable: my time with my family was far more valuable than my own pride. I decided that selfishly seeking the prideful moment was not worth the cost. Interestingly, it was shortly after that moment of realization that I found myself standing in a room with Saddam Hussein. The moment I became content to go the rest of my life without such a defining event is the moment God allowed me to experience one.

While the life lessons for me were enormous, the results of the mission on OBJ Abalone and a subsequent mission on OBJ Crosse were huge successes for U.S. forces and TF-121. Nine enemy fighters and terrorists were taken off the target and detained. One was an improvised explosive device (IED) technician for Al Qaeda. In addition to enormous amounts of RPGs, other weapons, and ammunition, the unit found nineteen IEDs in various levels of construction. Many, being made from concrete, were still wet. The British SAS soldier who gave his life on that mission probably saved untold others.

Just a week later, I flew down to Babylon for premission planning. The United States was considering a takedown of Muqtada al-Sadr, the controversial Muslim religious leader. Our base of operations was to be a small flight area near Babylon. Al-Sadr, leader of the Mahdi Army based in Najaf and deployed throughout southern Iraq, had incited numerous attacks against coalition forces and even established a shadow government in the place of the Iraqi Governing Council. U.S. leaders felt that removing al-Sadr was at least an option worth investigating. While the operators and aviators were planning their portion of the mission, I needed to assess the medical capabilities of the forward surgical team, which was located near where the assault would take place. I hopped a ride on a regular army helicopter bound for Babylon.

As we made our final approach, the ruins of the place were clearly evident. Babylon was built on either bank of the Euphrates River and became one of the largest cities in the ancient world. The hanging gardens of Babylon are listed as one of the seven great wonders of the ancient world. Today, only fallen and crumbled ruins remain. Some rebuilding has taken place to show the order and structure of the former city. The U.S. military was chastised for building a small helicopter landing area so near the ruins. I touched down on this airfield in early November and set about finding the medical unit located there.

The physician's assistant assigned to the facility was present and gave me a rundown of their capabilities. This forward area surgical team was well equipped with two general surgeons and had a healthy supply of blood products. These were the type of questions I usually asked when conducting premission planning. Should our operators be hurt, I needed to advise the command where to take the casualties. In cases where there were multiple wounded operators, decisions had to made on where to direct the wounded based on their injuries and the capabilities of the various units surrounding the area of the operation. For each mission, the medical planner would know the exact locations of all the med units in the area, and their capabilities, to include things like units of blood on hand. It was my job to gather that information and ensure the pilots knew how to get in and out of each of these facilities. I was essentially gathering info on the troops available portion of the METT-T analysis I discussed earlier. After gathering my intel, I enjoyed some brick-oven pizza made by the soldiers. My ride back to the base at Baghdad—a regular army medical evacuation helicopter—was happy to see me delivering pizza. We left Babylon well fed and wondering what the place looked like in its prime.

Many of the missions involved a lot of planning, only to have the mission canceled. In the case of al-Sadr, President Bush decided not to take him down. It was articulated to us that going forward, the U.S. wanted to partner with people like al-Sadr in hopes they would join a peaceful partnership governing Iraq. In retrospect, there is no way to know what might have been if we had grabbed the leader of the Mahdi Army. As with many of the canceled missions, we will just never know. For me, it was a nice trip to Babylon, and the pizza made it worthwhile.

Chapter Ten

The King of Babylon

The cascade of missions that followed, and which I described earlier, culminated in the capture of the Ace of Spades on December 13. As the door to his holding area was unlocked and I walked into the room to sit with Saddam, I could never have imagined what was to come over the next few hours. My only hope was to be there and witness a small piece of history. Still, I knew even as I sat down in the room that my involvement was at the hands of my Creator. At this point, I was unaware of my parent's recruitment of others to pray and fast. But I knew somehow that God had granted me an extremely unique opportunity, and I supposed it was because I had decided not to be consumed by the desire for just such an opportunity.

The room in which Saddam was being held was quite familiar to me, having done physicals on the HVTs taken prior to the arrival of the other physician. There were very few guards outside the room. The room itself had white ceramic tile up the walls and had a drain in the center of the floor. There were no holes in the walls for showerheads and no marks on the floor for a toilet, so our assumption was that it had been a kitchen in years past. In many Iraqi buildings, there is a separate room for preparing the food and then a separate place to cook the meal. This room had no markings where a stove or other cooking mechanism was located, so food preparation was probably its sole original purpose. In the corner of the room, an army cot now occupied the position where a table had been in my previous visits. Lying in the cot was the former President of Iraq, Saddam Hussein. The interpreter who had helped us with Saddam's secretary just a few weeks before greeted me and motioned to a folding chair. Saddam was trying to sleep, so I eased quietly in, sat down, and started to process where I was.

The "terp," whom I will call Joseph, had become a friendly acquaintance. I liked him because he was a Muslim but very pro-American. On one occasion, as I was waiting my turn to do physicals on an HVT, another interpreter described what Joseph was telling the HVT. He was, in fact, lecturing his subject. Joseph went through how the United States had supported Muslim fighters in their war against the Soviet Union. Joseph also mentioned the United States feeding thousands of Somalis during the famine there. He expressed how the United States had fought on the side of the predominantly Islamic Albanians against the Serbians and commented briefly on how the United States had gained concessions from Israel in the ongoing debate over the fate of the Palestinians. Further, Joseph had been the interpreter and interrogator for the hobbit. No interrogator wants a detainee to die during questioning, even from natural causes, which clearly the hobbit's illness and ultimate death was. My medics and my saving of the hobbit's life, if only for a brief moment, removed the stigma of his death from the interrogators and earned us a great deal of respect and appreciation in Joseph's eyes.

Saddam Hussein was lying in a green army cot about five feet from me, with a red cotton comforter pulled up to just under his chin. He was clean-shaven by the time I got to him. I recall he had his hand over his eyes and was trying to sleep. Joseph and I began a conversation about Islam. He and I had many of these talks in the weeks prior to this last night together. I had studied Islam in 1986 while spending several weeks living in the Pakistani section of Toronto, Canada.[1] For me, that experience was designed to give me a perspective on living in a foreign culture. Little did I know that the things I learned there would help me bond with Joseph and many others like him over the years.

As we talked, Saddam sat up; really, he bolted up, startling me, and asked me in Arabic to take his blood pressure. He gestured at me as if I were his caddy on a golf course, repeating the gesture until I stood next to him. He knew I was a physician; the stethoscope around my neck was a dead giveaway. I walked over and did so, not really making any other comments. As I placed the blood pressure cuff on his arm and inflated it, he gave me a lengthy, visual inspection. He did not lock eyes with me, choosing to look away when I attempted to match his gaze. There was an air of superiority at this moment; his facial expressions seemed to suggest that he saw me as his doctor to order around. I restrained a laugh at the thought that Saddam might feel anything but superior. Despite the air of aristocracy and his current situation, he seemed very relaxed. I, of course, was not. Here I stood, taking the blood pressure of one of the world's most wanted bad guys, wondering if he had any at all or if it flowed ice cold in his veins. Unlike so many of the other Iraqi HVTs, Saddam was not filthy. My medic Rob had already shaved him and cleaned him up a bit. I distinctly remember him not smelling. All the other HVTs had an odor of what I thought was curry mixed with sweat.

Saddam's demeanor, like his hygiene, had apparently changed significantly over the past few hours. When initially extracted from his hiding spot, Saddam was dumbfounded, per the Special Operations shooters who pulled him from his hole. He was quickly hooded and then flown from the target to a safe house on a Special Operations unit's compound. By the time he got to the compound, Saddam had apparently found himself again. Many of the operators came out to see him brought in. As they did so, an unintended cordon was formed, and Saddam passed through these men who were a part of this historic capture. Saddam's hood was removed as he was passed through this crowd of shooters. He began yelling, "I am the president of Iraq!" and, "You will pay for your crimes!" He even spat on one of the shooters, who very professionally maintained his composure and allowed the man to pass unmolested. I have no doubt that Saddam knew any physical marks on him from rough treatment would only aid his cause. But the shooters remained amazingly professional, and Saddam looked well cared for in the video that would soon be released to the world. The humane treatment of one of history's most murderous dictators further reveals the unprecedented pursuit of constraint by the U.S. military.

The unit then prepared him for transport to the battlefield interrogation facility on Task Force 121's main headquarters compound, my home at BIAP. I never learned how he was transported from the Tikrit area to Baghdad, but I assume it was by wheeled vehicle. Once he arrived at the main facility, Saddam had calmed down considerably. He was compliant with all directions. He was searched again, and he received the physical exam by the SOAR Medic Rob and my Special Operations doctor acquaintance. To them, he seemed as if he was back in a disbelief mode. Apparently, Saddam's megalomaniacal tendencies had convinced him he would never be captured. By the time I got to him, he was requesting a repeat blood pressure measurement. He seemed to be most concerned about his health. That impression would change over the course of our conversation.

Sitting back down, he returned to his supine position and I to my chair. After a few minutes of conversation with Joseph, who sat across the table from me in the little holding cell, I reached in my pocket, removed my disposable camera, and took a photo of Saddam lying in the cot. He sat back up again, startling me a bit. Saddam's cot was about five feet from me and at a ninety-degree angle to the table where I took notes through my interview. He did not seem annoyed by my photo, which was the last of a large number taken with him and of him that night. I was still suppressing the giddiness of being where I was at that moment. I thought, "Damn, I just snapped a photo of the butcher of Baghdad on a Kodak disposable." I wondered what the gal back at the photo lab would think of that. Saddam then asked Joseph the direction of Mecca. Unlike all Muslim peoples, Saddam did not kneel to pray; he stood from where he was seated on the bed, spun an empty chair facing the direction Joseph indicated, and bent slightly forward at the waist. As he prayed I was struck by the contradiction of it all. First, Saddam seemed to apply the rules of Islam differently to himself. He did not kneel or lay prostate on the floor. Saddam had tortured and killed hundreds of thousands of people, mostly with the sole purpose of consolidating and maintaining his own grip on power. Unlike the barbaric murders of the jihadists, who kill for a fanatic belief, Saddam had murdered and killed people who believed just as he did, only to preserve his own station in life. The image of the little Kurdish child dead in the arms of his dead mother following Saddam's use of chemical weapons, or "special mission with special weapons," immediately flashed in my mind.[2] But now, here he was praying to God. To me, it was unsettling. As he finished, he turned and faced me. He had an odd smile on his face as if he was about to tell me something I would find amusing. Speaking in Arabic through Joseph, he mentioned that at one time in his life, he had wanted to be a doctor. This began a five-hour conversation that changed my life.

The intelligence officer in the room was asleep. No one had given me any instructions not to speak with Hussein. Here he was starting a conversation, so I thought, "Why not?" I asked him what had attracted him about being a doctor. He recounted escaping from prison following his second coup attempt (his words). Saddam, a zealous member of the radical nationalistic Ba'ath Party, attempted to kill the king of Iraq, Faisal II, in 1956.[3] I believe this is what Hussein referred to when suggesting a first coup attempt. In 1958, a non-Ba'athist group of Iraqi army officers led by General Adbul Qassim and rivals to the Ba'ath party, were successful in ousting the king.[4] In 1959, Hussein and a group of Ba'ath party associates were unsuccessful in a daylight machine gun ambush of General Qassim.[5] The attack failed, but his involvement catapulted Saddam to senior leadership of the Ba'ath party. Historical accounts note that Hussein was wounded in the gunfight and that he escaped to Syria for medical attention.[6]

In the escape, Hussein was shot in the leg. Saddam recounted to me that the bullet entered his thigh from the inner margin and passed through in front of the femur. It exited on the outer side of the thigh. Saddam related the details to me of extracting the bullet himself. He was very animated describing his Rambo-like field surgery, pointing to the wound area covered by his pant leg and physically demonstrating how he removed the bullet. He very humanly grimaced, showing his teeth and squinting his eyes, remembering the pain of it all. Historically, there is very little information on why Hussein participated in these events. I asked Hussein why he got involved with the Ba'athists and specifically why he participated in the attempt on Qassim's life. Hussein responded that the Ba'athists were the party most dedicated to the independence of Iraq. He said, "And nothing mattered more to me." From the looks of the Iraq I saw, littered with palaces used only for Saddam and extreme poverty elsewhere, I doubted that last statement. He continued that his desire was for Iraq to be free of colonial influence and a leader among the "nations of Islam." Looking at the thousands of pictures and statues of Saddam throughout the country, it is difficult to accept that Hussein had any agenda other than Saddam. Yet the possibility exists that his early involvement was as idealistic as he recounted to me. We will never really know exactly when Hussein became so enamored with himself. Saddam did say, toward the end of his recounting of the injury and the attraction for medicine that it had caused, "Politics had a stronger pull on my heart." He laughed as he said this. So Hussein gave up the thought of being a physician in order to be a politician. Probably a better choice for the patients of Iraq, because I cannot imagine Saddam Hussein taking the Hippocratic Oath.

After his escape from prison, Saddam fled to Syria, where he found a friend who nursed him back to health. He did not say how long he stayed in Syria, and biographies on Hussein differ. There are some that say he spent up to four years in Syria. Others report trips, and some, a complete relocation to Egypt.[7,8] Saddam recounted to me that he stayed in Syria only long enough to heal from the injury. He told me he then moved to Egypt, where he met and developed a friendship with Egyptian President Gamal Abdel Nasser. Saddam suggested that Nasser kindled his love of politics. President Nasser was known throughout the world as an ardent Arab nationalist. Nasser was the coleader of the Egyptian revolution of 1952, removing King Farouk I and heralding a period of profound modernization and industrialization of Egypt.[9] This advancement for an Arab state produced for Nasser a cultish following in the Arab world, still only twenty-nine years from the final collapse of the Ottoman Empire, the last great Islamic republic. He inspired pan-Arab revolutions in Algeria, Libya, Iraq (Ba'athist), and Yemen.[10] He also played a role in the formation of the Palestinian Liberation Organization (PLO).[11] Even though he suffered humiliation at the hands of Israel in the crushing defeat of the Arab armies during the Six Day War of 1967, many in the Arab world view Nasser as a symbol of freedom and a man who brought dignity to a people struggling for self-esteem.

Most historians do not recount that Saddam had the kind of relationship with Nasser that Saddam told me he had. The predominant belief is that Nasser knew of Saddam and approved of his nationalist tendencies.[12] In many respects, some of the actions taken by Saddam were very similar to those taken by Nasser. He did overthrow a West-leaning government, drift toward a relationship with the Soviet Union, start wars that he ultimately lost, lead the nation of Iraq to a very developed status for certain segments of its society friendly to the Ba'athists, and fight to establish dominance in the Middle East. Yet Saddam never garnered the respect of the Arab world. From a brief review of the history of Nasser, what I know to be true from my tours of Iraq, and my studies of and my meeting with Saddam, Nasser acted on behalf of Egypt. Hussein acted on behalf of Saddam. And therein lies the difference that has led to such a polar opposite view of the two men in the Arab populace.

Why Saddam would even mention Nasser in this conversation with me sheds some light into Saddam's psyche. I got the distinct impression that the Ace of Spades was concerned about his image and how the world perceived him. His mentioning Nasser probably was meant for the interpreter. At several points in our conversation, I often wondered if Saddam was talking to me or to the people with whom I would share this account. At various points in our conversation, I felt as if Saddam talked unreservedly with me as a physician, that my being "only a doctor" gave him a candor he might not otherwise have shown to interrogators. I wonder if his demeanor would have been different if I had mentioned that I was previously an infantryman and a Ranger. In retrospect, I just do not know. He could very well have been playing me, giving me information that might cast a perception about him to the world, especially the Arab street. He then became rather coy and positioned himself as a president might when giving an interview to an historian. It was surreal.

Saddam also mentioned to me that since he had decided to pursue a career in politics, he opted to receive a degree in law. He mentioned that he got this degree while living in Egypt. I am not sure if it was the excitement of the moment, but I failed to ask him from which school in Egypt he had gotten his degree in order to verify it later. However, in General Georges Sada's book he recounts that Saddam graduated from a school of law in Iraq.[13] I did find reference to Saddam attending Cairo University School of Law but never finishing. Again, Saddam's story could not be corroborated. The thought that Saddam had convinced himself that certain falsehoods were true would arise for me at several times in the conversation. Saddam was either a very good liar, or like most liars, he became a believer in the stories he told. In that moment, I felt the latter was far more likely. But truthfully, Saddam was an excellent liar. In 1963, a group of Ba'ath party army officers killed General Qassim, along with all of the leaders of his government. Seeing this on the news (it was actually shown on the Iraqi evening news in all its gruesome detail), Hussein hurried home to join the revolution.[14]

My primary interest in the conversation remained on Syria at this point. The fact that Saddam was nursed back to health near the infamous Bekaa Valley, home to numerous terrorist organizations, made me wonder what kind of connections he had there now. The story of the dam break and his use of civilian airliners to move his chemical weapons were unknown to me at the time of our interview. However, it seemed only intuitive that Saddam might maintain friendships with people there who could serve his evasiveness on the question of special weapons. So I asked him, "Do you still have friends in Syria?" In my mind, I was thinking, "OK, tell me who your buddies are and where in Syria are they hiding the smoking gun?" His answer to this question was in stark contrast to all the other questions I asked that night. For every other question, Saddam would pontificate. All his answers were extraordinarily lengthy; he was a wordy man who would often express numerous positive attributes of himself when answering and often take the opportunity to talk about himself. However, when asked about his friends in Syria, Saddam just sat there. He said nothing, and his facial expression and affect were flat. I asked again and he said, "I've lost touch with them," and he again went silent, no smile. It crossed my mind that I did not want to be responsible for fouling any investigative work of the real interrogators, and I wondered if further questioning was probably getting too close to the line. I rededicated myself to avoiding any questions that might interfere with the investigations regarding WMD or any other possible war crimes.

I then asked Saddam what President Nasser was like. Saddam seemed to gleam when he described Nasser. He voiced that Nasser was a leader of all the Arab peoples and that his power came from his passion. Apparently, Nasser felt a duty to restore a certain degree of respect to the Arab people lost with the intrusions of the West. Saddam felt Nasser's greatest quality was his ability to pull all Arabs together. Saddam would later refer to Nasser as a great leader. But for now, he stopped short at that compliment. Taken in context of rumors that Saddam often felt that he himself was the return or reincarnation of Nebuchadnezzar, the King of Babylon, it seemed Saddam was still trying to associate himself with people who in Arab history had been great unifiers of the Muslim peoples. This unification of the lands of Islam is an attractive selling point to jihadists who feel the need and obligation for all Islam to unite in war against the infidel. Saddam's association with "unifying" leaders of the past fits the rumors and fits what many believed to be his personal quest to unify all Muslims under his leadership. The question remains: were Saddam's motives for such unification a religious zeal or merely a hunger for more power? For me, the answer to that question was obvious from the numerous effigies of Hussein on nearly every building and street corner and the fact that no Islamic governments rose up in opposition to his ousting. Clearly, the latter was far more likely than the former explanation.

Saddam's demeanor had relaxed significantly by this point in our discussion, and I found myself caught up in the moment. He was speaking exclusively through the interpreter in Arabic, and he did so throughout my time with him. I never knew if he could understand my English. He looked at me whenever I spoke but always looked to Joseph the interpreter when he repeated my questions in Arabic. I had relaxed as well, and we were speaking as nonchalantly as old friends. However, it was not a conversation. At this point, I was asking all the questions, and he was answering like some great dignitary being interviewed for a historical work. I sat at the table perpendicular to Saddam's bed. He had faced me, sitting cross-legged on his cot, and I had turned my chair to face him. Saddam rarely shifted his body position; it was as if he was posed for a painting. It came to mind that he had been extremely charming to this point in the conversation. The United States military sends its aviators and Special Operations people to interrogation resistance training, so I was aware to some extent that Saddam may have been similarly trained and might be working me, or manipulating me in some way. I distinctly remember reminding myself at this and other moments in my interview of him that Saddam had personally murdered people and had ordered the deaths of thousands, perhaps hundreds of thousands. To keep myself in check through the interview, I reminded myself of the torture of children he was reported to have done to extract confessions from opposition leaders. At certain points in the conversation, as I felt myself becoming enamored by him or the situation, I would remind myself of his many atrocities. I later discovered the following quote about Saddam from a general who knew him well:

> He was truly a genius at doing evil. He was a man with no conscience. He was ruthless and brutal, and there was nothing he wouldn't do to achieve his own ends. He killed many times and ordered the brutal murders of hundreds of thousands of our own people. He was a true Stalinist, inside and out.[15]

I was glad I kept my emotional distance. However, his charm and the excitement of this meeting meant I had to consciously keep myself from being caught up in the unprecedented moment.

I then asked Saddam how he became president of Iraq. Having read numerous books about him prior to the war, I was at least aware of the historical version. According to that version, within a few years of the death of Qassim, Saddam barged into the prime minister of Iraq's office, that of Abdurazzaq al-Nayif, pointed a gun to his head and advised him to choose asylum or death.[16] Al-Nayif wisely chose asylum, and Ahmed Hassan al-Bakr thus became president, prime minister, and minister of defense of Iraq. He appointed Saddam Hussein as his deputy. Saddam lived contently under al-Bakr until 1979 when, again at gunpoint, he offered al-Bakr the same options he had given al-Nayif.[17] Al-Bakr chose as al-Nayif to keep his life and thus fled Iraq. Hussein's official rule as president began.

Saddam apparently saw the story somewhat differently. He spoke to me about his love for al-Bakr. Saddam used the word father to describe his relationship with the president of Iraq with whom he had served since 1968. Saddam expressed that by 1979, al-Bakr had grown tired of leading the nation and had, over the previous few years, given Hussein much of the authority. From negotiating with neighboring Iran and other international relations to policing the internal affairs of state, Saddam said he was essentially doing all the work. He said that al-Bakr approached him in 1978 about assuming the senior position and expressed that Saddam was the clear choice to lead the nation. Saddam suggested that he voiced reluctance, but he noted that he ultimately "had to put the people of Iraq first and do his duty to the nation." His voice and his demeanor as he recounted this story was that of a humble servant. I thought his version was unlikely, but I moved on to my next question: "Why did you start a war with Iran?"

Saddam smiled and gave me a very interesting answer. His next few comments were perhaps the most revealing for me from the entire discussion. Saddam said that as early as 1975, he and Ruhollah Musawi Khomeini negotiated a deal the details of which I certainly have not heard revealed elsewhere. After three stints in an Iranian jail for protesting the Shah of Iran's Western-leaning policies, Khomeini fled Iran and settled in the second-most holy site for Shia Islam, Najaf, Iraq.[18] Khomeini, as do most Muslims, felt that the separation of church and state was unacceptable and in direct conflict with the teaching of the Koran. His concept of government was based on the notion that only clerics could dispense the Islamic law of sharia in an unbiased fashion. His opposition to the shah in the early 1960s set the stage for an eventual power struggle in 1979, which the shah lost.

Saddam related, matter-of-factly, that in 1975 he met with Khomeini on several different occasions and that his purpose for the meetings was to negotiate when the ayatollah would leave Iraq. Saddam was concerned that Khomeini's presence could incite the Shia, who were and are a majority of the population in Iraq. Khomeini had a different purpose: to remain close to Iran, where he could influence the religious fervor that would ultimately overthrow the shah. Saddam informed me that Khomeini had intentions of returning to Iran and establishing a theocratic state. Saddam did not specifically say that Khomeini expected to rule Iran, as he ultimately did; however, I took his answer as implying just that.

In order to appease Saddam, Khomeini offered him a deal. Once the shah was removed and the religious leaders were established in Iran, Iran would cede coastline and ports to Iraq, giving it a larger influence in the region by gaining additional access to the Persian Gulf. It is worth noting that at this point Hussein himself was not the president of Iraq. He would not unseat President al-Bakr until 1979. So in effect, this negotiation was between Khomeini, who hoped to rule Iran some day, and

Saddam, who at least in title was still only second in command of Iraq but who clearly had his sights set on the top slot in the government.

In 1978, for reasons that are not perfectly clear, Saddam expelled Khomeini from Iraq. I can think of two possible reasons, neither of which I can support. Clearly, Khomeini's growing influence with the Shia was a perceived threat to Hussein. It is also very possible that Saddam was prompted by Western governments, who felt that getting Khomeini as far from Iran as possible might help the political survival of the pro-Western shah. Many conspiracy theories suggest that intelligence services of the Western democracies were a part of Saddam's ascent to power. But Saddam did not speak of them. Either or both of these two possible explanations could clearly have weighed on Hussein. How Saddam's actions impacted Khomeini is easy to conclude. Once in power, Saddam told me Khomeini never honored his promise. On several occasions, Saddam said he attempted to raise the discussion with Khomeini, but the cleric never again spoke to him of this negotiation. Consequently, Saddam, who needed the additional access to the Persian Gulf, used this broken promise to justify the attack and devastating war with Iran.

There was a significant pause in our conversation, and I took the moment to soak in what Saddam was telling me. The thought that these two men had brokered an unwritten deal was something I had never read or heard. Saddam quickly jumped into the void. He added that it was his duty to the world to attack Iran. I thought, "Duty? That's a bit of a stretch." He explained without me having to ask that Iran's vast coastline on the Persian Gulf gave it a regional advantage. This advantage was now in the hands of what Hussein believed was a religious fanatic who was destabilizing to the world. He specifically said he attacked in order to ensure that the theocratic state of Iran would not tip the regional balance of power too favorably in its benefit. Clearly, the Shia presence in

Iraq, and Khomeini's connections with them, worried Saddam. I knew that Hussein had used chemical weapons on the Iranians and wanted to ask him about them. But again, my fear of fouling the impending interrogations concerning WMD caused me to pass. Instead, I asked Saddam if he believed he won the war with Iran, and he very honestly reported, "No one won the war." I was surprised by the admission. In Baghdad, there is a parade area for Saddam's soldiers to march by as he stands and inspects. The reviewing stands line a street that is approximately a mile long, with enormous crossed sabers serving as arches on either end. Protruding like cobblestones in the pavement, Hussein had buried the helmets of thousands of Iranian soldiers killed in the Iran-Iraq War. Essentially, his parading soldiers would be walking on the heads of dead Iranians. I never suspected that a man who would construct such a parade field would ever admit anything other than total victory. However, his downtrodden facial expression gave some credibility to at least his believing what he was saying.

I then turned my questions to Kuwait, asking, "Why did you invade Kuwait?" Saddam's answer had several parts. He began a very interesting discussion of how the area between the Tigris and Euphrates rivers was the site where mankind was born. The first humans, Saddam informed me, were created by God and placed in Iraq. He did not mention the Garden of Eden, although all three major monotheistic religions believe essentially the same creation story. The divisions of these religions come later in their history. He then suggested that since all human beings had their origins in what is now Iraq, all human beings were essentially Iraqi. I asked him if he was justifying invading Kuwait because they were Iraqi and he said essentially yes. Attacking them was not attacking another country. They, and everyone on the planet, are essentially Iraqi.

He proceeded, despite my attempts to interrupt him to get clarification on his statement, to explain the other reasons for his invasion of Kuwait. He was very matter of fact. He sat forward in his chair and used his right hand as a gavel in his left palm. With the index finger of the right hand extended, he patted his left palm as he "educated" me on the facts. In the months prior to the invasion, Saddam had approached the Kuwaitis on a number of occasions, arguing that the northernmost oil field in Kuwait was actually a part of Iraq. The border between Kuwait and Iraq was in dispute prior to and even after the fall of the Ottoman Empire. The modern-day border was established in 1913 and accepted by Iraq in 1932.[19] Prior to that time, the border was continuously contested. Iraq reaffirmed its commitment to the border when the Ba'athists came to power in 1963. Unfortunately for Kuwait, the Ba'athist leader at the time was not Saddam. Further, Saddam noted that for some time, the Kuwaitis had been directional drilling, or side drilling into the Iraqi oil fields, which he thought was stealing from the Iraqi people. Lastly, Saddam went on to say that the Kuwaitis, during his negotiations with them concerning the field's ownership, offered him $30 billion to keep the border where it was. Visibly upset even discussing it, Hussein emphatically recounted how this "offer to buy him" deeply offended him. The furrowed brow and lengthy sigh seemed animated as he related that his attack on Kuwait was an act to save his honor and his reputation.

I then asked Saddam if the invasion went as he planned, and I added, "Why did you stop at the southern border? Why not go on into Saudi Arabia?" Hussein said it was never his intention to even take all of Kuwait. His generals met such little resistance that they, on their own volition and against his instructions, continued the attack, capturing the entire county. He stressed his plan was only to take the northern oil fields. He repeated this at least three times: "I did not want to control all of Kuwait." But once it was done, he stayed. He again mentioned the fact that all humans are really Iraqi because Iraq is the cradle of civilization. Knowing what happened to people who disobeyed Saddam I found his disobedient generals story a bit of a stretch.

I asked Saddam if he expected the Americans to respond as they did, drawing a "line in the sand" and ultimately going to war to eject him from Kuwait. His answer surprised me. He said he fully expected the line in the sand. He also mentioned that he knew the American president would act, even if that meant war. Saddam expressed that he had miscalculated how long it would take the Americans to initiate an attack. He said his forces were ready in the early phases. He expressed a great deal of confidence in the Republican Guards to defend Kuwait had the Americans attacked within the first few months that his soldiers occupied their defenses. But he said, "I could not sustain my forces with them deployed so far from home." As the months of Desert Shield ebbed along, Saddam's army grew restless, and morale fell to precipitously low levels, along with food stores, fuel, and ammunition. Saddam said that by the time Desert Shield turned to Desert Storm, his men could not sustain the fight and were beaten. At the time, I felt the answer was genuine. It was certainly rational.

Because Saddam had clearly desired to be the next Muslim leader to unite all of Islam, I asked him how he felt about the Arabic countries that supported the coalition and the United States during Desert Storm. Contrary to what I expected, he was not angry. In fact, his facial expression showed a sort of ambivalence. He smiled and made a hand gesture to suggest that "such is life." He then began a rather lengthy discussion about the current leaders of the Arab states. He voiced that all served because of their relationships with the West and remained in power because wealth from oil revenues bought them the security forces to stay in power. He felt that had the Middle Eastern countries not grown fat and lazy from oil revenues, they all would seek to cooperate to defy the infidels. Saddam cited the Muslim concept of the "house of Islam," saying that the apostate leaders, meaning Western-leaning leaders of Islamic countries, were as much a threat to the house of Islam as the infidels. Again, I wondered if this was for the interpreter or whoever might hear of this account. While I could very well have been biased by my distaste for the man, his expressions of devotion to Muslim causes seemed fake to me. The house of Islam is similar to the Christian concept of the corporate church in one respect. All believers of Islam are members of the house of Islam. However, the house of Islam has significant differences in its corporate practices from those of the Christian church. For example, Christ compels believers to give unto Caesar what is Caesar's and give unto God what is God's.[20] He means there is a duty to both the civil government and the church, and the two are not one. As I understand Islam, the leadership of the government and of the church is the same, and the goal of most jihadists is that there be no government but that of the religion and that it transcends all nationalistic borders. In fact, most Muslims, according to Bernard Lewis in his work *The Crisis of Islam,* "tend to see not a nation subdivided into religious groups, but a religion subdivided into nations."[21]

What I believe Saddam was trying to do was connect himself to fundamentalist Muslims by criticizing the leaders of moderate Islamic states, who are preventing the union of all Islamic states into a truly unified house of Islam. After my interview and my travels throughout Iraq, I am certain Hussein would have eagerly volunteered as the leader of such a group. Actually, he would have felt compelled to accept the position, as it would assuredly be his by destiny and qualification.

Further, anyone not in the house of Islam is a member of the house of war, meaning that if you are not in the house of Islam you are at war with the house of Islam.[22] Saddam was known as a masterful twister of truth. Even in retrospect, I am not certain if Saddam believed what he was saying. The life he lived reflected a significant pagan lifestyle, encouraging others to worship him more than Allah and his Prophet Muhammad.

Yet in these first moments of capture, it seemed to me he was attempting to cultivate the image he wanted held for posterity.

The accusation Saddam made against apostate leaders and their wealth seemed a bit hypocritical. In my many months in Iraq, I stood in a number of his seventy-plus palaces. It was common to see marble floors, marble walls, gold-walled showers, sixty-foot-high crystal chandeliers, hand-carved wooden doors two stories high, and entire ceilings of hand-painted French and Italian frescos. A Fox News special estimated that Saddam had spent $2.2 billion on forty-eight palaces built since the end of Desert Storm in 1991.[23] The innumerable statues and paintings of Hussein made me wonder if he was really making the accusation against them or himself. Saddam's history of attacking the extremely fanatical religious state of Iran made it clear to me that a desire to unite all of Islam was second to his remaining in power. However, this prompted my final line of questions, beginning with, "So do you consider yourself a devout Muslim?" He was never able to answer the question.

About this time, roughly 5 AM local time, approximately five hours after my interview began, the admiral in charge of TF-121 came in the room and realized that Saddam was chatting nonchalantly with me. I believe he comprehended the freedom with which Saddam was speaking with me as a physician. He asked, "What's he talking about, doc?" I assured the admiral I had stayed away from any sensitive questions that might interfere with any investigation and that I was asking questions like "Why did he invade Iran?" The admiral said to me, "Doc, we've got to get this on tape." He ran from the room, and in a few moments, a communications expert arrived with a video camera and microphone on a stand. The cameraman then left the room. At that moment, and without hesitation, Saddam sat back in his bed, returned to a supine position, and pulled the covers over his head, thus effectively ending our conversation. All night long, he sat and eagerly answered almost all of my questions. Saddam was an aged man and had by this time been up for nearly twenty-four hours, showing no signs of fatigue. He enjoyed me asking the questions, and he certainly relished giving me his answers. But when the camera was connected, Saddam ended the interview.

Sometime just before this terminating event, the Special Operations surgeon who did the original physical exam on Hussein returned to the room. He was dozing in the back corner. With him in the room, I was free to leave. In fact, my replacement, Andy, the regimental surgeon, was due in that night, and I was expected to return with the plane to the States. Andy had graciously offered—as a servant leader would—to do the stretch over Christmas. Getting back to my area was essential in order to pack my gear for a departure that was scheduled only ten hours from that moment. Since Hussein was no longer talking, I said my good-bye to Joseph the interpreter and left the room. Walking back to my bunk area, I wondered if anyone would ever believe what just happened to me.

When I arrived back in my small room at the medical aid station, my home for this last trip to Iraq, I grabbed a couple of cold beverages and sat down to process it all. My room was a converted closet large enough for only a cot and a wall locker. I pulled the small army issue hardcover notebook from my laptop case and began writing down the details of my conversation. I had taken copious notes on the cover of the *Stars and Stripes* newspaper I took into the room with me. To say I was overwhelmed by the emotions of the moment would be an understatement. The only word I could find, both then and now, to describe it is "surreal." A mixture of excitement was clearly present; we had accomplished our main objective. I had a blend of emotions, but perhaps the strongest was the simple jubilation of winning. Like the Super Bowl champions, TF-121 had accomplished an amazing victory. We won; Saddam lost. That success made us all absolutely jubilant. For me, it was the added appreciation of the moment in history. I could not believe

I was a part of it. A murderous dictator who had operated on the international scene for thirty-plus years had been apprehended. His reign of terror was over. I wondered how quickly the world would forget this moment, but I knew that at least for now, this was very special, and I was unable to even voice my appreciation for being allowed to participate. As icing on the cake, I was going home to spend Christmas with my family.

Yet we all knew full well that the growing jihadist movement would keep our forces, and our special task force, in Iraq for some time. I finished the beverages about the time I finished journaling the conversation and tried to catch a few minutes of sleep before packing for home.

After a brief two-hour nap, I arose, packed my gear, grabbed some food, and sat down in our TV room to catch the news. Our medical area had an enormous television with stadium-style seating. One of the interpreters, not Joseph, sat in the room with me as we tuned in for the announcement to be made to the world.

Sometime Sunday morning in Baghdad, a military spokesman mentioned that a press conference was planned for later in the day. He mentioned an "important announcement" would be made and that there had been arrests, one of which was a "high value target." Immediately, the press began speculating and all the networks started broadcasting the possible arrest of the Ace of Spades, Saddam Hussein. The first official announcement came from Ambassador Paul Bremer. Bremer addressed a large group of journalists and Iraqi officials. I remember very clearly watching him approach the podium with a grin stretched from ear to ear. The first words from his mouth were, "Ladies and gentlemen, we got him!" Bremer's speech is provided in an attached appendix. I also remember very distinctly the uproarious crowd and the chants for Saddam's death. This, too, was surreal: watching the news conference, seeing the images and video of Saddam, and knowing I had just walked out of his cell after a five-hour conversation with him. The feeling was eerie, a mix of elation and also of fear because it meant a change in mission and not an end to the mission.

At 12:15 Sunday afternoon, President Bush came on television and addressed the nation and the world. The tyrant was gone. Saddam was in custody. President Bush's comments are also in a separate appendix at the end of the book.

Immediately following the announcements and particularly the images of a confused Saddam Hussein, conspiracy theorist hit the airwaves with numerous theories. Many Muslim people, who were looking for Saddam to give them a sense of self-respect against the infidels and were hoping for him to act like his sons, who had fought to the death, were shocked and in disbelief that Hussein was captured without a fight. Many suggested that an insider somehow drugged him and then led the infidels back to where Hussein was hiding.[24] Saddam was not drugged. He was not captured by the Kurds and then remanded to the Americans. He was not found by the United States 4th Infantry Division, although soldiers from that great outfit established blocking positions to keep people out while the army's elite counterterrorism unit assaulted the target.

Saddam was doing everything to keep from being found. In fact, his hiding place was excellent. The spider hole in which he had placed himself had been allegedly walked over by at least one operator. He was discovered when the sweep of the area was repeated. Imagine you are hiding, squatting in a hole about four feet deep and about three feet wide at the top. The lid to your hole is ripped off and the gun barrel of a Special Operations modified M-4 assault rifle is stuck three inches from your head. The knee jerk response of every human being on earth is to drop your weapon, and as a popular rap song says, "Put yo hands in the ayer, a ayer." No one shoots back in those circumstances. It was not drugs, just a natural human reaction, period, end of conspiracy.

As I continued to listen to the commentary and see the replay of the medical examination and the images from the target, I realized my plane home was landing within an hour. I ran back to my room, where I haphazardly tossed everything into my bags. I shucked my magazines of ammunition and handed them off to the medics, who would give them to my replacement. I handed my night vision goggles to the medics as well and loaded my gear on the hooptie. The smell of burning feces wafting from the battlefield interrogation facility, a smell we endured every night as the Iraqi prisoners burned their fecal matter with diesel, made me glad I was leaving Iraq.

After a last check inside for any of my gear, I said good-bye to my medics and walked outside. As we were pulling out in the Nissan pickup my friend from the 82nd had given us on my first few nights in Baghdad, the medical officer of the army's counterterrorism unit pulled up in his vehicle. He got out, handed me a bottle of Johnny Walker Green Label, and thanked me for my service to his unit. We talked only briefly, and then I headed down to the flight line to wait for the plane. Within a few minutes of my arrival, the plane touched down. In the grassy area between the two runways, a disabled DHL commercial transport plane hit by a jihadist's missile only a few months prior still sat unrepaired as the air force C-17 taxied toward us.

My replacement stepped off the aircraft. It was Andy, the regimental flight surgeon, my senior medical leader in the regiment, and a boss of sorts. While LTC Jeff was my direct boss, Andy gave all the physicians in the regiment both mentorship and direction as we served in our physician capacities. Andy and I exchanged some quick info on what to expect and the details of the previous day's mission. I was glad to be turning the care of the unit over to Andy; he was an extremely talented emergency medicine physician, trained at one of the best emergency medicine residency programs in the country and an experienced Special Operations flight surgeon. He had seen combat in the early parts of Operation Enduring Freedom, including the missions in Tora Bora and Operation Anaconda. With a nod and wave, I climbed aboard what the Vietnam Vets called the freedom bird and said good-bye to Iraq for the last time.

With Hussein caught, TF-121 renamed itself again and moved back to Afghanistan in full force. In March, only sixty days after getting home, I launched to OEF for my first experience in the Hindu Kush. Multiple missions searching for America's other most wanted, Osama Bin Laden, were to no avail. My most eventful experience in OEF was the death of Pat Tillman. The mission the night he was killed was more frightening than most. As I was climbing aboard the aircraft to support the Rangers insertion on an extremely high peak, my senior medic on the ground patted me on the back and said, "You must be a bit anxious going into the area near where those guys were shot down in Operation Anaconda." There is nothing like saying, "Hey, you are going back to where some guys were shot down" to set the tone of a helicopter mission.

After we placed our Ranger element on their hilltop, we did our obligatory race tracks in the sky a few miles from the target, waiting to see if there were casualties. We heard that one of the Ranger elements inserted by other means than our choppers had taken some casualties. I recall the pilots initially planning to move to the wounded soldier, but before the move could be initiated, the call came that the soldier was KIA. In the air that night, we diverted and picked up an Afghani casualty who had a survivable injury. Only later would I be told that the Ranger who died that night was none other than the NFL football player Pat Tillman. I will never forget the almost half-mile-long cordon formed by army Rangers and special operators as his flag-draped casket was carried to an awaiting

C-17 for the long flight home. The portrait of Pat's brother, kneeling at the casket as the doors to the C-17 closed is an image others have shared as their most unforgettable of the war. Rangers, some of the hardest men in our military, wept openly for a man they all admired, a man who had sacrificed a plush life to serve the nation he loved.

To this day, the 160th SOAR, and other U.S. military and federal agencies continue the hunt for Bin Laden, Al Qaeda terrorists, and many other fanatical terrorists. While it would be an absolute joy to see him captured, Bin Laden's wings are successfully clipped. He lives in some hole in Pakistan, a hole probably not unlike Hussein's. He is unable to move from the only part of the world where he can blend in and be hidden by a populace who cares nothing for the millions of dollars in reward and everything about any man who defies America. The men of the Special Operations task forces continue the valiant hunt, regardless of where they are asked to go. If you pray, remember the men who fly those choppers into hell looking for him, the operators they carry, and especially the medics who go where the shooters go in the effort to bring all of them back alive.

Epilogue

Final Thoughts

Following my assignment to the 160th Special Operations Aviation Regiment, I took a job as chief of emergency medicine at the army hospital at Fort Campbell, Kentucky. There I served out my remaining two years of active duty military service. On a spring morning in 2006, I was in my army uniform, making my way through the clearing process of getting out of the army. It was my last official task after sixteen years of active duty service, first as an infantry officer and later as an army emergency medicine physician. I had completed everything on the list except one remaining item. The last box needing someone's initials was at the transportation office. As I walked up to the building, I saw hundreds of Night Stalkers gathering at a large auditorium adjacent to the transportation office. Recognizing many friends, I walked up and asked what was going on. Tragically, two Night Stalkers had been killed when their MH-6 Little Bird crashed in Iraq. This was yet another memorial service. I postponed signing out and joined my friends in a tribute to two amazing warriors who had sacrificed all for the army, the nation, and our freedom. As I sat in the chair, I remembered the memorial ceremony at the Night Stalker monument the day I signed into the unit. That day marked my beginning in the nation's elite Special Operations community. And now, my last day in the army was equally marred by tragedy, another reminder of the cost of fighting this war.

It was a moment for reflecting. I was leaving the one organization to which I had given my entire adult life. July 1982, on the sun-scorched plain at West Point, I took the oath to defend the constitution of the United States of America against all its enemies. In that place, men like George Patton and Douglas MacArthur had stood as cadets and taken a similar oath. Now, some twenty-four years later, I was walking away for good. As General MacArthur would say late in his life, "Like the old soldier ... just fade away." Again, though, the ending was punctuated with the sacrifice of two brave men. As I sat listening to the various speakers relate with suppressed tears the lives of these two pilots, my mind reflected back over my years of service in the army. All I could think about were the people, the men and women who, for a period in time, shared with me in the honor of wearing the uniform of a U.S. soldier. I remembered my radio-telephone operators, the guys who stuck to me like glue and carried the various radios that connected me to my men and my commanders when I was in command of various infantry units. Their faces passed through my mind like address cards in a Rolodex. These men shared foxholes, food, and laughs with me. Mostly, we shared a camaraderie that escapes prose. I remembered my driver when I was a young second lieutenant in the infantry. We called him Peewee; he was literally four feet and eleven inches tall, and as young as any new private. He was from upstate New York, with a heart as big as the Empire State itself. I remembered hundreds of others, sergeants and fellow officers. And of course, I remember the medics of the 160th SOAR. Their commitment to the men they served was unparalleled to any I had witnessed in all my years in the army. The images and memories of these men blurred and merged with the history of our army, Washington's men at Valley Forge, Darby's Rangers, the Screaming Eagles in the Ashu Valley of Vietnam, and on and on. My thoughts of fellow brothers and sisters in arms, and my connectedness with those of the nation's past, made me proud. We made very little money, but we worked with a conviction that ours was a higher calling. We believed in America and in its unique place in history. As taps played for the two Night Stalkers lost, I wept not only for them, but also for my own departure from this unique fraternity.

In considering the people of the army, I thought again about Pat Tillman. Pat's life ended in a dusty valley in Afghanistan. He was the tragic victim of a friendly fire incident. Lately, the controversy surrounding his death has garnered all the attention about this man. Like the two 160th SOAR pilots being memorialized, it is my belief his death did not and should not define him. When we think of Pat Tillman, we should learn from the mistakes of friendly fire, and the fact that fratricide is inevitable should not keep us from diligently preventing it. However, Pat Tillman should be remembered for walking off a field in Phoenix and onto the Ranger training fields and the nation's battlefields. His legacy is his decision to exchange the shoulder pads for body armor. Or even more noteworthy, the millions of dollars and a plush lifestyle he gave up for the sands of the Middle East. His was a choice to stand up against tyranny abroad, a real, murderous, brutal tyranny that left hundreds of thousands dead and millions more deprived of basic freedom.

Thoughts of tyranny and brutality led me to my night with Saddam. At the time of the memorial ceremony, Saddam was still alive, waiting the second of two trials for crimes against humanity. To me, Saddam was a man who would do anything to gain and retain power. His life was about himself and no one else. The psychopathology of Saddam is beyond even my clinical abilities, but few in the history of the world, even Adolph Hitler, match his ruthless rise to power. His cruel and brutal acts to retain that power were more heinous. Saddam allowed nothing to stand in the way of his quest for power and for greatness. In the end, he was caught by the world's most elite special operators, and met justice at the end of a rope. His quest to be the next Nebuchadnezzar, uniting the Arab world, failed. I considered the countless lives sacrificed by him for his own greed. I am thankful for the part I played in his coming to justice.

The contrast between Tillman, and everyone in the U.S. military, with Hussein is remarkable. Pat sacrificed his financial status as a professional football player. He knew when he walked away from football that his opportunity to be a Hall of Fame player was over. His quest for greatness, something that fuels almost all athletes, was surrendered to the call to serve his nation. Saddam, on the other hand, let not even the lives of people stand in his way. His megalomania consumed him, and ultimately it destroyed him. Pat died in sacrifice to the freedom of others. Saddam died for depriving others of their freedom. Saddam took from others for his personal gain. Pat gave all he had for the sake of others and his country. "No greater love ..."

As the ceremony continued, my thoughts drifted to the life lesson I learned while there. Differently than Hussein, my Halloween night experience in 2003 made me realize the quest for a great defining moment was not worth the risk of missing my children growing older, or missing a life with the wonderful woman God gave me. My pride took a back seat to the valuable people in my life and the convictions of my creator. Saddam, on the other hand, never learned the lesson. And in the end, he paid the price for it, as his sons, misguided by his quest for power, gave their lives defending his tyranny, and he died a brutal death at the hands of his accusers. I did not resolve to leave the army for fear of death; I was still very much committed to the cause and to my duty to serve. But for me, I let go of the desire to be anything more than what fate allowed, and I resolved to give my life to the cause my God created me for, and nothing more. Interestingly, I now believe it was at the moment I surrendered my pride that God allowed me the experience of a lifetime.

Lastly, I considered this war to which so many — these two men among them — had given the ultimate sacrifice. There are people now who live in freedom because of the sacrifices of America's men and women in arms. And while we all acknowledge mistakes were made, each challenge facing the military was ultimately overcome. The initial invasion was a huge success. The insurgency was crushed following Saddam's capture. Al Qaeda's involvement ended with al-Zarqawi's death. The sectarian violence was beaten down by the surge. Despite the declaration of its failure by Congresswoman Nancy Pelosi and Senator Harry Reed four days before the last troops set foot in Iraq, the surge brought a peace to Iraq it had not seen in decades. More importantly, the overall American effort gave Iraqis the right to choose their own destiny. The soldiers, sailors, airmen, and marines have something to be proud of. As the final benediction for the memorial services ended, I hugged a few men and Night Stalker families, walked off Fort Campbell, Kentucky, and out of the U.S. Army.

My greatest fear, considered that day as the memorial ended and almost daily now, is that some Americans and much of the Western world may never understand the nature of the Global War on Terror. The jihadists in Pakistan and Yemen, and the theocrats in Iran, are bent on continuing the fight regardless of what our media and our liberal academics say about America. Radical Islam adheres to the following global vision statement:

> Islam is not a normal religion like the other religions in the world, and Muslim nations are not like normal nations. Muslim nations are very special because they have a command from Allah to rule the entire world and to be over every nation in the world. Islam is a revolutionary faith that comes to destroy any government made by man. Islam doesn't look for a nation to be in better condition than another nation. Islam doesn't care about land or who owns the land. The goal of Islam is to rule the entire world and submit all of mankind to the faith of Islam. Any nation or power in this world that tries to get in the way of that

goal Islam will fight and destroy. In order for Islam to fulfill that goal, Islam can use every power available every way it can be used to bring worldwide revolution. This is jihad.[1]

Written in 1970 by Mawlana Abdul Ala Mawdudi, the founder of the Pakistani fundamentalist Islamic movement, this clearly articulates the ultimate goal of the jihadist movement.

The goal is evident everywhere in the Islamic world. Following the bombings in London in 2005, a Palestinian cleric spoke on Palestinian television, saying "we must annihilate the infidels and the polytheists, your enemies and the enemies of the religion. God count them and kill them to the last one, and don't leave even one."[2] This goal is taught at a very young age. Jordanian textbooks for children in middle school states, "This religion [Islam] will destroy all other religions through the Islamic Jihad Fighters."[3] Simply put, radical Muslims believe that to kill nonbelievers advances Islam's domination of the world. The ultimate goal is clearly world domination. This is not hyperbole. They shout it from their pulpits and they broadcast it in the classrooms. Radical Islam seeks world domination. Period.

These proofs confirm to me the never-ending nature of this war. As long as there is a youth in a madrasas in Pakistan chanting, "Death to America," the War on Terror will not end. This is a challenging realization, but it is not incorrect. Even President Barack Obama's gracious attempts to salvage a relationship have failed. Bin Laden and Iranian leader Mahmed Ahmadinejad continue to mock him and flagrantly continue their efforts to destabilize and ultimately destroy us. Resolve in this conflict must take on the same meaning as the resolve to fight crime on the streets of any U.S. city. It is a daily fight that will continue for generations to come.

Perhaps the most concerning aspect of all is a nuclear Iran. This is unfathomably frightening. In fact, it is to me the singular most challenging event in the history of man. Many nations have, in the past sixty-three years, acquired nuclear weapons. Numbered among this elite club is even North Korea. And while they frequently rattle their sabers, even Kim Jong Il is not suicidal. However, the radical jihadists are just that. Suicide bombs take on a new meaning when they are measured in megatons. The ability to have a million or more souls lost in a split second means it is an absolute necessity to prevent the radical anti-American state of Iran, which fosters and equips terror agents to execute suicide attacks, from acquiring any nuclear technology. Any objection to this strategic imperative is lunacy.

I realize articulating the unending nature of this effort is hard for many Americans to accept. The disappointment and anticlimatic nature of an unending campaign does not negate the wisdom of continuously pursuing the campaign. One man with a bomb can kill hundreds. They hate us and will stop at nothing to bring about their desired world vision. However, our success hinges completely on the willingness of the American people to pursue these criminals to the ends of the earth. Political expedience needs to be placed to the side for the greater good. We need to support the continued and unfortunately unending need to prosecute this war. Interestingly, the media attempted early on to make comparisons between OIF and Vietnam. There is one area where a comparison is accurate, and that is the impact of the media on the will of the nation for the fight. Thus victory hangs in the balance.

Former North Vietnamese General Staff Officer Bui Tin once said that the peace movement was "essential to our strategy." "Visits to Hanoi by people like Jane Fonda and former Attorney General Ramsey Clark gave us confidence that we should hold on in the face of battlefield reverses.... Through dissent and protest, it [America] lost the ability to mobilize a will to win."[4]

We stand at a precipice in the War on Terror. Iran is more than saber rattling. Al Qaeda is down but not out. Interestingly, Hillary Clinton, who ultimately lost the democratic nomination for president, made pulling out of Iraq central to her candidacy during the primary. She was quoted early in the war as saying on *Meet The Press* in regards to setting a timetable for withdrawal, "I think that would be a mistake....We don't want to send a signal to the insurgents, to the terrorists that we're going to be out of here at some, you know, date certain. I think that would be like a green light to go ahead and just bide your time."[5] Early on, Clinton voiced an understanding that, with visible dissent, the enemy, like the North Vietnamese, could have confidence to hold on in the face of battlefield losses. Then, when she needed the support of the Democratic Party in order to be its candidate for commander-in-chief, she seemed to expediently lose an understanding of the concept. Now, Secretary of State Clinton is supporting a delayed withdrawal. Dissecting the flip-flop on the issue, and the need to do so to be elected, is important but not a part of this book. What is true is that the enemy will continue to look for weakness among our leaders, and Clinton's flip-flop on the issue will surely not be helpful as she operates as our secretary of State. I can hear the Hamas leaders now, "She is the one who said not to pull out and then later changed her mind for political expediency's sake. All we have to do is continue the fight." The enemy will look for more Hanoi Janes in America to sustain its will to fight.

The war will be won or lost in the living rooms of America as the will to fight the war strengthens or ebbs away. Should the will be affected by those looking to differentiate themselves from a party or leader, the subsequent loss of the war will be on their heads. Failing to stay the course will be a travesty for the many lives lost and the tens of thousands who returned with wounds and scars for life.

Saddam Hussein is dead, and my involvement in the direct action is now over. For me, the quest for a defining moment became an important life lesson. The mission on Halloween 2003, where the enemy was only feet from where our helo landed, to rescue the British SAS operators made me realize that life was not about a quest for defining moments. I let it go, and only a few days later, I flew as the medical support to the nation's most elite Special Operations force as it captured Saddam Hussein. I then spent the night with the King of Babylon on the first night of his capture. God seems to know how to get us exactly where he wants us.

It has been my pleasure, and my distinct honor, to serve with some of the greatest Americans who have ever lived. The pilots, crews, support staff, and especially the medics of 160th Special Operations Aviation Regiment have profoundly impacted our national security and the freedom of people across the globe. They are my brothers and sisters in arms, and I will always feel the loss of leaving them to continue this fight without me.

While we trade cards of great baseball players, the real heroes of the day march, ride, or fly humbly to do battle on our behalf. They risk it all for the sake of our freedom. They suppress fear, and live with stress on the family back home, and they go where they are ordered. Their families endure the separation and the potential loss of their husband, wife, father, mother, son, or daughter. They endure it despite the pain and despite the challenge. They conjure up images of American warriors of old, and they press on. Many have made the ultimate sacrifice, and many more, the amputees and paralyzed, will pay the price daily for the rest of their lives. If we do not love them, and tear up at the thought of their amazing sacrifices, then we are lost. But any withdrawal prior to the completion of the effort is a slap in their faces and a dishonoring of their sacrifice. The greatest honor we can give these men and women is our continued support of their defense of us against a radical ideology that seeks our subjugation or our death.

OBL remains at large, but largely ineffective. Iran now looms as the greatest threat in the war on terror. For me, like most Americans, I look on from the sidelines and watch the Night Stalkers and other army friends continue the fight. I feel like I am peering through the window, watching the events unfold on the other side out of my reach, and I pray for their safety. But more importantly, I pray the American people stay the course. As in the wars of our past, when committed Americans support their soldiers, we never lose. In the global fight against terror, there is no other option.

Appendix A

Selected References

Chapter 3: Who Are the Night Stalkers?

[1] Helis.com Helicopter History Site.
http://www.helis.com/featured/eagle_claw.php.

[2] Pushies, F. *Night Stalkers: 160th Special Operations Aviation Regiment (Airborne)*. The Military Power Series. Zenith Press, 2005.

[3] "Invasion of Grenada."
Wikipedia.http://en.wikipedia.org/wiki/Invasion_of_Grenada.

[4] Pushies, F. *Night Stalkers: 160th Special Operations Aviation Regiment (Airborne)*.

[5] Ibid.

[6] Durant, Michael J. and Stephen Hartov. *The Night Stalkers*. The Penguin Group, 2000. 112–159.

[7] Pushies, F. *Night Stalkers: 160th Special Operations Aviation Regiment (Airborne)*.

[8] Ibid.

[9] Bowden, Mark. *Black Hawk Down*. Atlantic Monthly Press, 1999.

[10] "Executive Summary of the Battle of Takur Ghar." Release by Department of Defense, 24 May 2002, 1–2.

[11] "Operation Anaconda." Wikipedia. http://en.wikipedia.org/wiki/Operation_Anaconda.

[12] "Executive Summary of the Battle of Takur Ghar," 4.

[13] Ibid., 6.

[14] Corey, Senior Medic, 160th SOAR (A). "Presentation to Special Operations Medical Personnel," Fall 2003.

[15] Durant, Michael J. and Stephen Hartov. *The Night Stalkers*.

[16] Corey, Senior Medic, 160th SOAR (A). "Presentation to Special Operations Medical Personnel," Fall 2003.

[17] Durant and Hartov.

[18] Ibid.

[19] Corey, Senior Medic, 160th SOAR (A). "Presentation to Special Operations Medical Personnel," Fall 2003.

[20] "Executive Summary of the Battle of Takur Ghar," 10.

Chapter 5: Combat Preparations

[1] Lionel Giles. *Sun Tzu On the Art of War*. Project Gutenberg's eBook #132. http://www.gutenberg.org/files/17405/17405-h/17405-h.htm.

[2] Ibid.

[3] Broad, William J. and Judith Miller. "Traces of Terror: The Bioterror Threat; Report Provides New Details of Soviet Small Pox Accident," *New York Times*, June 15, 2002. http://query.nytimes.com/gst/fullpage.html?res=9B06E2 DF103CF936A25755C0   A 9649C8B63.

[4] Miller, Judith. "Threats and Responses: Germ Weapons; C.I.A. Hunts Iraq Tie to Soviet Small Pox," *New York Times*, Dec. 3, 2002. http://query.nytimes.com/gst/fullpage.html?res=9C0DE4 DD163BF930A35751C1A9649C8B63.

[5] Hilts, Phillip J. "Deaths in 1979 Tied to Soviet Military," *New York Times*, Nov. 18, 1994. http://query.nytimes.com/gst/fullpage.html?res=950DEF D71331F93BA25752C1A962958260.

[6] Rangwala, Glen. "Briefing Notes on UNSCOM Interview with Hussein Kamel," *Iraq Watch*, Feb. 27, 2003. http://www.iraqwatch.org/perspectives/rangwala-kamel-022703.htm.

[7] Ibrahim, Youssef M. "Iraqi Offers Regrets in Killing of Defecting Sons-in-Law." *New York Times*, May 10, 1996.

[8] Bush, George W. State of the Union Address, Jan. 2003. http://www.whitehouse.gov/news/releases/2003/01/20 030128-19.html.

[9] Ann Coulter, *Godless; The Church of Liberalism*. New York: Three Rivers Press, 2007. 114.

[10] Ibid., 124.

[11] Ibid., 114.

[12] Dave E. Lounsbury and Patrick W. Kelley. *Military Preventive Medicine: Mobilization and Deployment*, Military Medical Textbooks, Vol. 1. Borden Institute, Washington, D.C.: Walter Reed Army Medical Center. 23. http://www.bordeninstitute.army.mil/published_volume s/mpmVol1/PM1ch2. pdf.

[13] Patton, John F., et. al. "Metabolic Cost of Military Physical Tasks in MOPP 0 and MOPP 4." Technical Report, Army Research Inst. of Environmental Medicine, Natick, MA, April 1995. http://handle.dtic.mil/100.2/ADA294059.

14 Technical Report, "Assessment of Performance of Tasks by Personnel Dressed in Chemical Protective Clothing." Technical Analysis and Information Office, U.S. Army Dugway Proving Ground, Dugway, Utah, June 1987. 1.

Chapter 7: Finding the Bad Guys

1 "Intelligence Community Assessment of the Lieutenant Commander Speicher Case." Department of Defense, 27 March 2001.

2 "Mohammad Zaidan." Wikipedia. http://en.wikipedia.org/wiki/Abu_Abbas.

3 Clancy, Tom and Gen. Carl Stiner. *Shadow Warriors*. New York: G.P. Putnam's Sons, 2002. 266–296.

4 Ibid.

5 "Muhammad Zaidan." Wikipedia. http://en.wikipedia.org/wiki/Muhammad_Zaidan.

6 Sada, Georges and Jim Nelson Black. *Saddam's Secrets: How an Iraqi General Defied and Survived Saddam Hussein.* Brentwood, TN: Integrity Publishers, 2006. 254.

7 Ibid., 259.

8 "Izzat Ibrahim Al-Douri." GlobalSecurity.org. http://www.globalsecurity.org/military/world/iraq/al-douri.htm.

9 "Charles-Édouard Brown-Séquard." Wikipedia. http://en.wikipedia.org/wiki/Charles-Édouard_Brown-Séquard.

10 "'Mrs. Anthrax' Surrenders to U.S. Military." FoxNews.com. May 5, 2003. http://www.foxnews.com/story/0,2933,85990,00.html.

Chapter 10 - The King of Babylon

[1] This was a program designed to teach people how to integrate with people of different faiths and from different cultures. We essentially lived in the Pakistani section of Toronto, learning both Islam and the culture.

[2] "Iraq's Kurds Uncertain Factor in U.S. Coalition: Ethnic Minority Long Persecuted by Saddam Hussein." CNN.com/World. 27 Nov. 2002. http://images.google.com/imgres?imgurl=http://i.cnn.ne t/cnn/2002/WORLD/meast/11/27/sproject.irq.kurds/ku rds.iraq.chemical.weapon.jpg&imgrefurl=http://www.cnn .com/2002/WORLD/meast/11/27/sproject.irq.kurds/ind ex.html&h=168&w=220&sz=11&hl=en&start=2&um=1&tb nid=ud1CnbgONLJ2_M:&tbnh=82&tbnw=107&prev=/ima ges%3Fq%3Diraqi%2Bchemical%2Bweapons%2Bkurds%26 um%3D1%26hl%3Den%26safe%3Dactive%26sa%3DN.

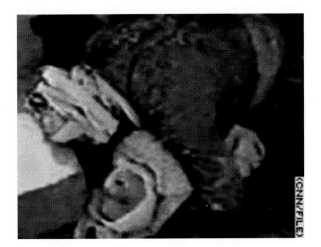

[3] "The Personal History of Saddam Hussein." Emergency Response & Research Institute (ERRI) EmergencyNet News Service, Counterterrorism Archive. http://www.emergency.com/hussein1.htm.

4 "Saddam Hussein." Wikipedia.
   http://en.wikipedia.org/wiki/Saddam_Hussein.

5 Shalom, Stephen. Znet. Dec. 15, 2003.
   http://www.zmag.org/content/showarticle.cfm?ItemID=
   4685.

6 Ibid.

7 "The Personal History of Saddam Hussein." Emergency
   Response & Research Institute (ERRI) EmergencyNet News
   Service, Counterterrorism Archive.

8 Shalom, Stephen, Znet. 1.

9 "Gamal Abdel Nasser." Wikipedia.
   http://en.wikipedia.org/wiki/Gamal_Abdel_Nasser.

10 "Saddam Hussein" Wikipedia, The Free Encyclopedia. 3.
   http://en.wikipedia.org/wiki/Saddam_Hussein.

11 "Gamal Abdel Nasser." Wikipedia.
   http://en.wikipedia.org/wiki/Gamal_Abdel_Nasser.

12 Gordon, Michael. "Faithful Choice on Iraq Army Bypassed
   Debate." *New York Times*, March 17, 2008.
   http://www.nytimes.com/2008/03/17/world/middleeast
   /17bremer.html?_r=1&oref=login.

13 "The Personal History of Saddam Hussein." Emergency
   Response & Research Institute (ERRI) EmergencyNet News
   Service, Counterterrorism Archive.

14 Ibid.

15 Sada, Georges and Jim Nelson Black, 13.

16 "Ba'ath Party Coup 1968." WebChron: The Web Chronology
   Project.
   http://thenagain.info/WebChron/MiddleEast/BathCoup.
   html.

[17] "The Personal History of Saddam Hussein." Emergency Response & Research Institute (ERRI) EmergencyNet News Service, Counterterrorism Archive.

[18] "Ruhollah Khomeini." Wikipedia. http://en.wikipedia.org/wiki/Ruhollah_Khomeini.

[19] "History of Kuwait." Wikipedia. http://en.wikipedia.org/wiki/History_of_Kuwait.

[20] Matthew 22:21, *The Bible*.

[21] Lewis, Bernard. *The Crisis of Islam*. New York: Random House, 2003.

[22] Ibid., 29–46.

[23] Donaldson-Evans, Catherine. "Saddam's Palaces are Tasteless and Tacky." Fox News, 16 April 2003. http://www.foxnews.com/story/0,2933,83854,00.html.

[24] Dr. Nimrod Raphaeli. *Conspiracy Theories Surrounding Saddam's Capture*. Middle East Media Research Institute, Dec. 19, 2003, No. 155.

Epilogue

[1] Mawlana Abdul Ala Mawdudi. "The Threat of Theocracy: Islam and World Domination, Breaking Spells." Dec. 9, 2007. http://breakingspells.wordpress.com/2007/12/09/the-threat-of-theocracy-islam-and-world-domination/.

[2] Palestinian Television Broadcast, July 8, 2005, presented on the DVD *Obsession*.

[3] Jordanian School Book, 1998, presented on the DVD *Obsession*.

[4] Bui Tin, interviewed by Stephen Young. "Examining the Myths of the Vietnam War, A Conference, Under the Auspices of

The RADIX Foundation." Boston: Simmons College. July 2004. 26–29. http://www.viet-myths.net/BuiTin.htm.

[5] Clinton, Hillary. *Meet the Press*. Sept. 23, 2007. http://www.msnbc.msn.com/id/20941413/.

Appendix B

Glossary of Terms

APU	Auxiliary power unit, a small jet engine used to power the electronics of aircraft while the main engines are shut down.
AQ	Al Qaeda
Augmentee	A regular army soldier who was temporarily assigned to the Special Operations task force but was not himself or herself a Special Operations soldier.
BIAP	Baghdad International Airport
BIF	Battlefield interrogation facility
Bird	Generic name for aircraft
BP	Battle position
Bumped	To be removed from a mission or aircraft
CASEVAC	Casualty Evacuation; any aircraft could become a casualty evacuation platform. This was often an aircraft also used as an assault platform but which was rigged with medical equipment for dual use. These aircraft did not have red crosses on them.
CENTCOM	Central Command

Combat Controller	An air traffic controller who accompanies special operators and controls fixed wing attack aircraft to assist ground assaults
CONPLAN	Contingency plan
CT Unit	Counterterrorism unit, the name I use for the army's elite Special Operations strike unit. I have chosen not to use the common name for this organization. They are still considered black "SOF" and while many people speak of them using their real name, I have chosen not to do so.
DAP	Direct action penetrator; an MH-60 Black Hawk rigged with forward-facing guns, rockets, and missiles, converting it to an attack helicopter
DNBI	Disease non-battle injury
FAST	Forward area surgical team
Grounded	When a pilot is taken off flight status and not able to fly; usually due to a medical condition that would impair either his flying skills or ability to egress in the event of a crash.
Hit	A term used to describe an assault on a target, often meaning an assault designed to grab a key person instead of seizing a piece of terrain or building
HVT	High value target, usually a person and not an item or facility
ISB	Intermediate staging base
IED	Improvised explosive device

JOC	Joint Operations Center; a planning and battle management headquarters for forces from more than one branch of the service
LZ	Landing zone
MEDEVAC	Medical evacuation; usually an aircraft that is always flown for the specific purpose of carrying wounded soldiers
MOPP	Mission oriented protective posture is the level of chemical protective equipment worn by a soldier; there are four distinct levels that add protection from one to four; MOPP-4 is every inch of skin covered and respirations are filtered.
NBC	Nuclear, biological and chemical; NBC designates training or personnel oriented on protecting the force during a WMD attack
NCO	Noncommissioned officer is an enlisted soldier who has risen to the rank of corporal or higher, essentially the foreman level of the army; these are the guys who get the job done
NEO	Noncombatant evacuation operation
NSDQ	The abbreviation of the Night Stalker motto: "Night Stalker's don't quit"
Night Stalker	Nickname for members of the 160th Special Operations Aviation Regiment
NVG	Night vision goggles
OBL	Osama Bin Laden
PEA	Pulseless electrical activity; the condition of a heart when the electrical pathways are

	still sending signals to the heart muscle, but the chambers of the heart are not contracting together to produce a pulse
PLF	Palestinian Liberation Front
PLO	Palestinian Liberation Organization
PDF	Panamanian Defense Force
PJ	Air force pararescue jumper
POTUS	President of the United States
PZ	Pickup zone
QRF	Quick reaction force
RDF	Rapid deployment force, a subset of a unit ready to deploy in a reduced amount of time due to the posture it is placed in when serving as the RDF
SOAR	Special Operations Aviation Regiment
Take Down	An assault on an enemy position; the term originated from the phrase "taking down a target"
Task Force (TF)	A temporary assemblage of different units combined for a period of time and given a specific mission
TOC	Tactical operations center; a subordinate unit's headquarters and planning areas and battle management center.
SOCOM	Special Operations Command
SOF	Special Operations forces
SOP	Standard operating procedure
WMD	Weapons of mass destruction

Appendix C

Transcript of Ambassador Bremer's Announcement

Ladies and gentlemen, we got him!

Saddam Hussein was captured Saturday, December 13, at about 8:30 PM local in a cellar in the town of ad-Duar, which is some fifteen kilometers south of Tikrit.

Before Dr. Pachachi, who is the acting president of the Governing Council, and Lt. General Sanchez speak, I want to say a few words to the people of Iraq.

This is a great day in your history.

For decades, hundreds of thousands of you suffered at the hands of this cruel man. For decades, Saddam Hussein divided you citizens against each other. For decades, he threatened and attacked your neighbors.

Those days are over forever. Now it is time to look to the future, to your future of hope, to a future of reconciliation.

Iraq's future, your future, has never been more full of hope. The tyrant is a prisoner. The economy is moving forward.

You have before you the prospect of sovereign government in a few months.

With the arrest of Saddam Hussein, there is a new opportunity for members of the former regime, whether military or civilian, to end their bitter opposition.

Let them come forward now in a spirit of reconciliation and hope, lay down their arms and join you, their fellow citizens, in the task of building the new Iraq.

Now is the time for all Iraqis—Arabs and Kurds, Sunnis, Shias, Christians, and Turkomen—to build a prosperous, democratic Iraq at peace with itself and with its neighbors.

Appendix D

Transcript of President Bush's Address to the Nation

Yesterday, December 13, at around 8:30 PM Baghdad time, United States military forces captured Saddam Hussein alive. He was found near a farmhouse outside the city of Tikrit, in a swift raid conducted without casualties. And now the former dictator of Iraq will face the justice he denied to millions.

The capture of this man was crucial to the rise of a free Iraq. It marks the end of the road for him and for all who bullied and killed in his name.

For the Ba'athist holdouts largely responsible for the current violence, there will be no return to the corrupt power and privilege they once held. For the vast majority of Iraqi citizens, who wish to live as free men and women, this event brings further assurance that the torture chambers and the secret police are gone forever.

And this afternoon I have a message for the Iraqi people: you will not have to fear the rule of Saddam Hussein ever again. All Iraqis who take the side of freedom have taken the winning side. The goals of our coalition are the same as your goals: sovereignty for your country, dignity for your great culture, and for every Iraqi citizen, the opportunity for a better life.

In the history of Iraq, a dark and painful era is over. A hopeful day has arrived. All Iraqis can now come together and reject violence and build a new Iraq.

The success of yesterday's mission is a tribute to our men and women now serving in Iraq. The operation was based on the superb work of intelligence analysts who found the dictator's footprints in a vast country. The operation was carried out with skill and precision by a brave fighting force.

Our servicemen and -women and our coalition allies have faced many dangers in the hunt for members of the fallen regime and in their effort to bring hope and freedom to the Iraqi people. Their work continues, and so do the risks.

Today, on behalf of the nation, I thank the members of our armed forces, and I congratulate them.

I also have a message for all Americans. The capture of Saddam Hussein does not mean the end of violence in Iraq. We still face terrorists who would rather go on killing the innocent than accept the rise of liberty in the heart of the Middle East. Such men are a direct threat to the American people, and they will be defeated.

We've come to this moment through patience and resolve and focused action. And that is our strategy moving forward. The War on Terror is a different kind of war, waged capture by capture, cell by cell, and victory by victory. Our security is assured by our perseverance and by our sure belief in the success of liberty. And the United States of America will not relent until this war is won.

May God bless the people of Iraq, and may God bless America. Thank you.

Recommended Further Reading about 160th
Special Operations Aviation Regiment

Black Hawk Down, Mark Bowden, Atlantic Monthly Press, New York. ISBN 0-87113-738-0

In the Company of Heroes, Michael J. Durant and Steven Hartov, G. P. Putnam's Sons, New York. ISBN 0-399-15060-9

The Night Stalkers, Michael J. Durant and Steven Hartov, The Penguin Group. ISBN 0-399-15392-6

Night Stalkers: 160th Special Operations Aviation Regiment (Airborne). The Military Power Series, F. Pushies, Zenith Press, 2005. ISBN 0-7603-2141-8

About the Author

Following graduation from West Point in 1986, Mark served as an Infantry Officer for over nine years. He left the military to attend medical school at Wright State School of Medicine in Dayton, Ohio, in 1995. His residency in emergency medicine was completed back on active duty at Fort Hood, Texas. In 2002, Mark joined the 1st Battalion, 160th Special Operations Aviation Regiment as its flight surgeon. In his two years with the unit, Mark deployed to OIF twice and OEF once. He was awarded the Combat Medics Badge, the Air Medal with "V" Device, and the Bronze Star. He currently serves as the president and CEO of MD-Partners, PLLC, a health-care company whose mission is to assist emergency departments and hospitals reach excellence. He can be reached at markegreenMD@gmail.com.